The 'Clash of Civilizations' 25 Years On

A Multidisciplinary Appraisal

EDITED BY

DAVIDE ORSI

E-INTERNATIONAL RELATIONS PUBLISHING

E-International Relations
www.E-IR.info
Bristol, England
2018

ISBN 978-1-910814-43-7 (paperback)
ISBN 978-1-910814-44-4 (e-book)

Production: Michael Tang
Cover Image: Samot via Depositphotos

A catalogue record for this book is available from the British Library.

E-IR Edited Collections

Series Editors: Stephen McGlinchey, Marianna Karakoulaki and Agnieszka Pikulicka-Wilczewska
Copy-editing: Cameran Clayton

Editorial assistance: Jakob R. Avgustin, Hayden Paulsen, Marianne Rozario and Andrei Sterescu

E-IR's Edited Collections are open access scholarly books presented in a format that preferences brevity and accessibility while retaining academic conventions. Each book is available in print and digital versions, and is published under a Creative Commons license. As E-International Relations is committed to open access in the fullest sense, free electronic versions of all of our books, including this one, are available on our website.

Find out more at: http://www.e-ir.info/publications

About the E-International Relations website

E-International Relations (www.E-IR.info) is the world's leading open access website for students and scholars of international politics, reaching over 3.5 million readers each year. E-IR's daily publications feature expert articles, blogs, reviews and interviews – as well as student learning resources. The website is run by a registered non-profit organisation based in Bristol, UK and staffed with an all-volunteer team of students and scholars.

Acknowledgments

I would like to thank all members of the E-International Relations team for their support and in particular Phoebe Gardner, Kurtis Edwards and Farah H. Saleem. I am very grateful to Cameran Clayton for her help in the production of this book. I am also indebted to Stephen McGlinchey for his constant support. I would like to thank all the authors for their patience and hard work.

Davide Orsi

Abstract

The purpose of this collection is to present Samuel P. Huntington's 'Clash of Civilizations' thesis, and to appraise its validity and shortcomings 25 years after the publication of his landmark article in the journal *Foreign Affairs*. The notion of a 'clash of civilizations' is examined from a multidisciplinary perspective and its validity is appraised in the fields of International Relations, European Politics, International Law, Political Theory, and International History. First, the volume examines Huntington's contribution from a theoretical perspective, focusing on his ideas about politics and the concept of civilization. Second, the articles collected in this volume also consider Huntington's thesis in the light of recent events in international politics, including the conflict in Ukraine, the rise of ISIS, China–India relations, the electoral success of far-right movements in Europe, the refugee crisis in the Mediterranean, and the activity of the International Criminal Court in Africa. This volume offers to its readers a vibrant and multifaceted conversation among established and emerging scholars on one of the most important paradigms for the understanding of international politics and the history of the twenty-first century.

Davide Orsi is an Editor-at-large at E-International Relations. His first book *Michael Oakeshott's Political Philosophy of International Relations: Civil Association and International Society* (Palgrave, 2016) explores the historical and normative dimension of international society by relating Oakeshott's philosophy of civil association to English School theories of international relations. He is also co-editor of *Realism in Practice: An Appraisal* (E-International Relations, 2018). He has published work in journals including the *Journal of International Political Theory*, *Collingwood and British Idealism Studies*, the *European Legacy*, *Filosofia Politica,* and the *British Journal for the History of Philosophy*. His research interests include international political theory and the history of political thought.

Contributors

Ravi Dutt Bajpai is currently a Doctoral candidate at Deakin University, Melbourne, Australia. His thesis is focused on civilizational aspects in International Relations and contemporary China–India relations. His research interests include international relations theory, ancient and contemporary social and political thoughts in post-colonial societies.

Gregorio Bettiza is Lecturer in International Relations at the University of Exeter. He recently completed a book manuscript exploring how religion has increasingly become a subject and object of American foreign policy since the end of the Cold War. Gregorio is the author of the 'Religion in International Relations' (2016) entry for the *Oxford Bibliographies*. He has also published articles in the *European Journal of International Relations*, *Review of International Studies*, *International Studies Review,* and *Politics* among others.

Glen M.E. Duerr is Associate Professor of International Studies at Cedarville University. A citizen of three countries, he has a Ph.D. in Political Science from Kent State University and is the author of *Secessionism and the European Union*, which was published by Lexington Books in 2015.

Ian Hall is a Professor in the School of Government and International Relations, Griffith University, Australia. His most recent book is *Dilemmas of Decline: British Intellectuals and World Politics, 1945–1975* (2012). He has published in various journals, including the *European Journal of International Relations*, *International Affairs*, and the *Review of International Studies*.

Jeffrey Haynes is Emeritus Professor of Politics at London Metropolitan University. He recently completed a book on the United Nations Alliance of Civilizations and is now writing another on *Twenty-Five Years of the 'Clash of Civilizations'*. He is book series editor of 'Routledge Studies in Religion & Politics'. He is also co-editor of the journal, *Democratization*, and its book series 'Special Issues and Virtual Special Issues'.

Anna Khakee is Senior Lecturer and Head of the Department of International Relations at the University of Malta. She has years of experience consulting international organizations, including the Norwegian Peacebuilding Centre and the United Nations Development Program (UNDP). She has published widely in international journals such as *Journal of North African Studies*, *Mediterranean Politics*, *Mediterranean Quarterly*, and *East European Politics and Societies*.

Jan Lüdert is Assistant Professor/Associate Program Director in the School of Applied Leadership at City University of Seattle, Washington. He is a scholar alumnus of the Liu Institute for Global Issues, an interdisciplinary research hub for emerging global issues at the University of British Columbia (UBC), Vancouver. Jan earned his Ph.D. in International Relations from UBC's department of Political Science.

Kim Richard Nossal is a professor in the Department of Political Studies and the Centre for International and Defence Policy at Queen's University in Kingston, Ontario. He is a former editor of *International Journal*, and served as president of the Canadian Political Science Association. His latest book, co-authored with Jean-Christophe Boucher, is *The Politics of War: Canada's Afghanistan Mission, 2001–14*.

Fabio Petito is Senior Lecturer in International Relations at the University of Sussex. He is the Scientific Coordinator of the Italian Ministry of Foreign Affairs-ISPI initiative on 'Religions and International Relations' and convener of the *Freedom of Religion or Belief and Foreign Policy Initiative*. Among his publications: *Religion in International Relations* (2003), *Civilizational Dialogue and World Order* (2009) and *Towards a Postsecular International Politics* (2014). Recent articles include: *"Dialogue of Civilizations in a Multipolar World: Toward a Multicivilizational-Multiplex World Order"*.

Erik Ringmar teaches in the Political Science Department at Lund University, Sweden. He has a Ph.D. from Yale University. He worked for 12 years in the Government Department at the London School of Economics and for seven years in China, for the last two years as professor of international relations in Shanghai. He is the author of five books and some fifty academic articles.

Anna Tiido is an Estonian diplomat and researcher. She has a master's degree in Sociology from Tallinn University, and one in International Politics from CERIS (Centre Européan de Recherches Internationales et Stratégiques) in Brussels. Her Ph.D. in International Relations is from the University of Warsaw. Her research is on the impact of the Russian minority issue on the relations between Estonia and Russia.

Wouter Werner is Professor of International Law at the Centre for the Politics of Transnational Law at the VU University, Amsterdam. His research focuses on the construction of international legal argument, with a specific focus on the use of repetition and testament of law.

Ana Isabel Xavier (Ph.D. in International Relations from University of Coimbra, Portugal 2011) is a Guest Assistant Professor at the Faculty of Arts and Humanities of the University of Coimbra (FLUC) and full Research Fellow at the Centre of International Studies (CEI-IUL). She also collaborates with the Research Centre of the Security and Defence of the Military University Institute. Ana Isabel Xavier is frequently invited to comment on international politics in Radio and Television of Portugal (RTP)

Contents

Introduction

DAVIDE ORSI

Over the past 25 years, Samuel P. Huntington's article 'The Clash of Civilizations' (1993) has shaped public opinion and the ways in which the academic world thinks about world politics. Events in the Middle-East and Asia, American military interventions, the Ukrainian conflict, the refugee crisis in the Mediterranean, Brexit, the rise of far-right movements in America and Europe challenge our traditional frameworks and seem to show the persistent relevance of the controversial notion of a clash between opposing and incommensurable values, religions, cultures and beliefs. That article, written in 1993, still seems to provide, in particular to the public opinion, a paradigm through which to interpret our times.

The purpose of this collection is to offer a critical analysis of Huntington's contentious ideas and to appraise its relevance to the understanding of today's political context. The book aims to be both a guide for students looking for an introduction to the notion of a 'clash of civilizations' and a point of reference for scholars interested in the debate provoked by Huntington's work. The collection does not present a single univocal interpretative line, but it rather offers different approaches and perspectives. Some contributors stress the persistent relevance of the 'clash of civilizations' thesis, others praise its importance for the study of international relations, others advance a strong and polemical criticism.

Already in 2013, E-International Relations published a collection on the 'clash of civilizations' to discuss Huntington's legacy (Barker 2013). Different from that book, this collection contains longer essays and has a stronger multidisciplinary character. Contributors have indeed considered the 'clash of civilizations' thesis from the point of view of different disciplines: International Relations, Political Science, International Law and Political Theory.

The Design of the Book

The structure of the book reflects this multifaceted and eclectic approach. A first series of contributions examines the theoretical content and legacy of

Huntington's ideas. Chapter one provides a sort of introduction to the thesis defended by Huntington in the 1993 article and in the 1996 book. To this end, it illustrates the philosophical root of their arguments by placing the theory of the 'clash of civilizations' in the context of the realist tradition in international political thought. In Chapter two, Ian Hall focuses on the concept of civilization by comparing Huntington's theory to Arnold J. Toynbee's. Hall underlines some of the similarities between the two thinkers, especially in their aims and assumptions, but also some of their important differences, with particular regard to their divergent accounts of the relationships and encounters between civilizations. In his essay (Chapter three), Erik Ringmar advances a much more polemical interpretation of Huntington's idea on the 'clash of civilizations', linking it to a quintessentially American way of relating to other civilizations.

In their contribution (Chapter four), Gregorio Bettiza and Fabio Petito consider the rise of discourses, institutions and practices built on the premise that civilizations and inter-civilizational relations matter in world politics. They show that the 'clash of civilizations' paradigm advanced by Huntington is not the only possible kind of civilizational analysis of international politics. Moreover, they defend the critical potential of civilizational approaches in a time of crisis of both national identities and liberal universalizing projects. Jeff Haynes (Chapter five) explores the relevance of Huntington's ideas for the understanding of the world after the end of the Cold War, and its importance for the 'return to religion' in International Relations. At the same time, Haynes highlights how in the years after 9/11, and also in response to Huntington's thesis, there has been a rise in attempts of inter-civilizational dialogues, which are now facing new challenges.

Paradigms wish to explain the world and there is no doubt that with his article and book Huntington wanted to offer an instrument for the understanding of international politics in the twenty-first century. Focusing on an often-neglected aspect of Huntington's work, Kim Nossal (Chapter six) examines the idea of 'kin-country rallying' and argues for its relevance to the understanding of international affairs. This notion, much less famous than that of clash of civilization, also characterizes Huntington's paradigm and claims that states are part of civilizations and behave like kin. This theory, argues Nossal, explains the relations among some countries much better than traditional international relations theory. In Chapter seven, Glen M.E. Duerr compares the predictions made by Huntington, Fukuyama and Mearsheimer on the world after the end of the Cold War, with particular regard to the rise of ISIS, the wars in the Middle-East, and the Ukrainian crisis. This latter case is of particular interest because Huntington seems to offer contradictory statements on the possibility of a conflict between Russia and Ukraine over Crimea and the eastern part of the country. The contribution by Anne Khakee

(Chapter eight) also examines the Ukrainian case and advances a criticism of Huntington's civilizational analysis. Khakee argues that the current crisis between Russia and Western powers can be explained by looking at them as clashes between alternative political systems, not civilizations. Chapter nine by Anne Tiido is also devoted to the case of Russia and of its foreign policy. Tiido instead underlines the role of the idea of civilization in Putin's discourses and actions as well as in Estonian political life after the end of the Soviet Union. These contributions examine the relationships between Russia and its neighbors, showing both their shortcomings and potential. Chapter ten, by Ravi Dutt Bajpai focuses on a non-Western context and on the relationships between China and India. Bajpai examines how the self-perception of being 'civilization-states' has shaped the national identities and bilateral relations between the two countries. Wouter Werner (Chapter 11) writes on an often neglected aspect when appraising the impact and the relevance of Huntington's thesis: that of its influence on the study of International Law. Werner considers this in the case of the actions of the International Criminal Court in Africa and explores how arguments about civilizations are used to counter cosmopolitan claims on human rights and international society. Werner shows that the idea of a 'clash of civilizations' is important in contemporary normative debate on international law and justice.

As already mentioned, Huntington's thesis has also had a huge impact on the public debate, especially over issues related to multiculturalism and relationships with religious minorities. In Chapter 12, Ana Isabel Xavier explores the current migrant crisis in the Mediterranean and its perceived link with a 'clash of civilizations'. She also considers the impact of this crisis on the policies of the European Union and on the future of the European project. In Chapter 13, Jan Lüdert sheds light on the use of the image of the 'clash of civilizations' by far-right movements in the European political context, by examining the electoral success of Alternative for Germany (AfD) in the 2017 German general elections. Lüdert offers a detailed account of the impact of Huntington's ideas on AfD's political position and rhetoric, with particular regard to the refugee crisis and the relationship with Muslim communities.

As is already clear from this short introduction, the volume offers a rich analysis of Huntington's ideas. It presents the most important arguments and ideas grounding the idea of a 'clash of civilizations', it examines the validity of that thesis for the understanding of international affairs and international law in contemporary world politics, and discusses its persistent relevance in the public debate.

References

Huntington, Samuel P. 1993. "The Clash of Civilizations?." *Foreign Affairs* 72, no. 3 (Summer): 22–49.

1

The 'Clash of Civilizations' and Realism in International Political Thought

DAVIDE ORSI

The thought of Samuel Huntington, and in particular his ideas in the 1993 article and 1996 book *Clash of Civilizations and the Remaking of World Order* (2002), have contributed to the conceptual vocabulary through which the changing international context has been examined after the end of the Cold War and the rise of Islamist terrorism. Huntington's central thesis that conflicts in the post-ideological era are fueled by differences in identity, religion or, more generally, culture (Huntington 1993, 22), has had a huge impact on the study of international politics. Some praised Huntington for his ability to forecast future trends in international affairs. After 9/11, some intellectuals even looked up to him as a prophet of the wars of the new century. In the US and in Western Europe, the notion of a 'clash of civilizations' between the West and Islam offered arguments to many intellectuals and activists, across the political spectrum, who saw in Muslim immigration and the geopolitical situations of Muslim countries a danger for a declining and confused West (among many others see Fallaci 2002). At the same time, Huntington has been loathed as the inspirer of a logic of 'us' versus 'them' that had some resonance in the policies of George W. Bush after 9/11. He has been accused of being ignorant of his own and other cultures, and to propose a static and caricature-ish description of civilizations, and in particular of Islam (Said 2001, Adib-Moghaddam 2010).

This chapter takes a different approach and starts from a different methodological presupposition inspired by the British philosopher and historian of political thought Michael Oakeshott. While trying to present to readers the political and moral thought of Thomas Hobbes, Oakeshott claimed that in order to understand a text in political philosophy one should place it in the context of the history of that discipline (1991, 223–228). In so doing, it would be possible to highlight those elements that escape from the contingencies and the darkness of the time in which philosophers were writing. Of course, in the case of a thinker so embedded in his time such as Huntington, it may appear as a bold claim to affirm the presence of theoretical elements of his thought detached from its time and place. At first glance, it seems that Huntington was more interested in offering advice to the American political elite, than to contribute to the theoretical understanding of international affairs. The questions that a book such as *The Clash of Civilizations* asks are indeed of a practical sort. However, as I hope to demonstrate in this short essay, it is possible to find in Huntington's theory of the 'clash of civilizations' some elements that are independent from the contingencies of his, and our, time and that can be linked to the history of the philosophical reflection on international affairs. These, I contend, are the elements that still appeal to readers from both the academic world and the general public.

Starting from this methodological presupposition, the aim of this chapter is to present and understand some of the main aspects of Huntington's argument as presented in the book and article on the 'clash of civilizations' (Huntington 1993, Huntington 2002). I claim that his thought can be seen in continuity with the realist tradition in International Relations and as one of the most prominent and strong critical critiques of utopianism in international political thought.

The Realist Tradition in International Political Thought

In order to show Huntington's contribution to realism, it is first necessary to offer a brief overview of that tradition. Realism is indeed one of the most recognizable voices in international political thought and is still holding center stage in the study of contemporary international affairs (see the contributions in Orsi, Avgustin, Nurnus 2018). Historians of international political thought agree in identifying two sorts of realisms: classical and structural. The former starts with Thucydides and continues with thinkers such as Machiavelli, Hobbes, E.H. Carr and Morgenthau (Boucher 1998, 47–170); the latter is instead influenced by the 'scientific approach' and aims to reach a quantitative and certain study of politics and is based on the notion of the balance of power (Mearsheimer 2013). My contention in this chapter is that while Huntington criticized some of the central tenets of structural realism, his theory of the 'clash of civilizations' can be seen in continuity with classical realism. To this end it is worth highlighting some of the main ideas that define the identity of classical realism in the philosophical reflection on international affairs.

Notwithstanding their many differences, classical realist thinkers shared a tragic vision of life (Lebow 2003; Rösch and Lebow 2017) according to which human beings have to take difficult decisions in a condition of uncertainty and with incomplete knowledge of reality. According to this view, all humans are embedded in changing contexts with no certain guide. This conception is linked to a profound critique of all forms of universalism, according to which it is possible, by the use of reason, to reach universal moral truths. The tragedy of the human condition also lies in its inescapability. Neither human reason nor universal moral law can come to the rescue of human beings.

At the same time, human nature is conceived of as self-interested. Human nature shapes the character of any human activity and, most of all, of politics. However, this condition is even worse in international politics. It is indeed in the international realm that the real nature of politics appears in all its force. For example, this fundamental idea is at the center of the political theory of one of the most important realist thinkers of the twentieth century: Hans Morgenthau. Writing at a time when International Relations as a discipline was not established as yet, Morgenthau's declared purpose was far from that of any scholar of our time: to find the eternal truths of politics (Morgenthau 1955). To this end, he applied to the study of politics the ideas of his teacher, the German legal philosopher Carl Schmitt. In Schmitt's *The Concept of the Political*, politics is conceived in terms of power. That this is the character of politics is well represented in the description of the state of nature by Hobbes. In the *Leviathan*, the state saves human beings from the constant threat of violent death: for Schmitt's Hobbes, the authority of the state derives from its ability to protect the citizens, who, in return, give their obedience. For Schmitt, there is no distinction between politics and war and indeed politics is the continuation of war by other means (Foucault 2003). The relations among states are characterized not by actual war, but by a constant state of belligerence in which the world is divided along the lines of friend/foe (Schmitt 2008, 37).

Conflict is a constant feature of human history, and of international history in particular. As Martin Wight famously put it, in international politics, no progress is possible and if some people from the distant past returned to present and looked at international affairs, they 'would be struck by resemblances to what they remembered' (Wight 1966, 26). As a consequence, as shown by Machiavelli (1988) but also by other realist thinkers, the only morality in politics is that identified with expediency and prudence and with the interest of the political community. Good politicians are those who protect their state and increase its power. In the absence of universal moral laws, the political woman/man should use her/his prudence to face difficult situations and 'to make a friend of every hostile occasion' (Oakeshott 1991, 60).

In addition to a tragic conception of human life, and the supremacy of power over ethics, realism in modern international political thought is also shaped by what Nicholas Rengger has recently defined as an 'anti-pelagian imagination' (2017). One of the characters defining this tendency is the aversion against the hope for universal moral truths (such as that about the existence of universal rights) to be a guide for political action. Moreover, anti-pelagianism fights against the belief that human history displays progress. Of course anti-pelagianism is not exclusively a character of realist international thought and many liberal theorists, starting with Judith Shklar, share distrust in utopian thinking (Rengger 2017, Chapter six). However, it is fair to say that the polemical targets of many classical realist thinkers were the utopian projects of their own times. If we look again, as an example, at Hans Morgenthau, we see that he criticized international liberalism in world politics. Its fault is not to acknowledge the centrality of power in politics and the ubiquity of evil in the world (1948).

To recapitulate, classical realist thinkers ground their argument on a tragic conception of human nature, and on the idea that international politics is essentially characterized by anarchy and war. Their positions often present a critique of utopianism and of the idea that international politics may be constrained by law or ethical principles, and is animated by a progress towards the best. In the following, I will illustrate the ways in which Huntington's theory of 'clash of civilizations' is related to these ideas.

Huntington's Critique against Structural Realism

As is well known, the main objective of Huntington's article and book on the 'clash of civilizations' was to offer a new paradigm to interpret world politics after the end of the Cold War. The historical events following the unexpected dissolution of the Soviet Union were redesigning world history and putting to the test established theories of international relations. Also inspired by Kuhn's *The Structure of Scientific Revolutions*, Huntington believed that the events such as the war in the Balkans and Chechnya showed the inadequate explanatory power of previous framework for interpreting and understanding world politics (Huntington 2002, 29–30). What was needed was a new paradigm and Huntington offered a new way of seeing international affairs grounded on the claim that 'the great divisions among humankind and the dominating source of conflict will be cultural' (1993, 22).

A first aspect to clarify is that this does not equate to saying that before the end of the USSR and during the Cold War culture and ideas were irrelevant or did not enter the equation explaining international conflicts. It rather means that the origin and reasons of war would not be the underlining competition between superpowers – a competition that during the Cold War was not just material, but also ideological – but rather the conflict between incommensurable ways of seeing the world and ways of life, those shaped by civilizations. In a sense, Huntington claims, civilizations have always been there: 'human history is the history of civilizations' (Huntington 2002, 40). This character of history was, however, hidden under the more apparent and manifest conflict between the two superpowers and their allies. My contention in this chapter is that this vision of world politics can be better understood when seen in the context of the realist and anti-pelagian tradition in international political thought. However, if we look at both Huntington's article and book on the 'clash of civilizations' we can see that one of their main concerns was to show the inadequate explanatory force of realism, and especially Mearsheimer's theory (Huntington 2002, 37).

According to Huntington, in realist theory 'states are the primary, indeed, the only important actors in world affairs, the relations among states is one of anarchy, and hence, to ensure their survival and security, states invariably attempt to maximize their power' (2002, 33). According to Huntington, this approach is able to explain the importance of states, it does not take into account the fact that states define their interests not just in terms of power: 'values, cultures, and institutions pervasively influence how states define their interests' (2002, 34). In the civilizational paradigm, states are still important, and power politics is still shaping their actions. However, these should be conceived within certain frames of reference: civilizations. These are 'a collection of cultural characteristics and phenomena', the 'broadest cultural entity', 'the highest cultural grouping of people'. There are some common objective elements that define civilizations 'such as language, history, religion, customs, institutions, and the subjective self-identification of people' (2002, 43). In the post-Cold War era, civilizations, and in particular their religious aspects, are the source of identity and meaning for a growing numbers of individuals and groups. Therefore, they shape the decisions of states and the study of international affairs should take this into account.

As many critics have noted, Huntington's definition of civilization is so vague and generic that it is useless in the actual analysis of world politics. However, the theoretical importance of Huntington's theory in this regard lies in his criticism of the realist paradigm and its focus on material interest and power as the driving forces of international politics. In contrast to that, Huntington sees a 'cultural reconfiguration of global politics' (2002, 126), in which a country's enemies and friends are defined by cultural identity. In a sense, power and interest still guide international agents, but these are defined by cultural framework. There is a priority of culture over interest and power.

The fact that agents define their interests through the vocabulary and ideas offered by their civilization is not the only aspect of structural realism that is criticized by Huntington. The 'clash of civilizations' paradigm explains the rise of non-state actors such as regional organizations. These, as well as alliances between states, are more and more shaped by civilizations. In the post-Cold War era, states suffer 'losses in sovereignty, functions, and power' (Huntington 2002, 35) in favor of these larger entities. For example, in the case of the European Union, states, which committed to an 'ever closer union', despite the many problems and setbacks, have progressively given up their economic, military and juridical powers to the institution of the Union. In the 'clash of civilizations' paradigm, the essence of the European Union is cultural homogeneity (Huntington 2002, 28), which is ultimately grounded in Christianity. The fact that 'people rally to those with similar ancestry, religion, language, values, and institutions and distance themselves from those with different ones' (Huntington 2002, 126) also explained the entrance of new states into the European Union after the collapse of the Soviet Union. The civilizational paradigm is not recognized in the founding documents of the European Union and, in particular, in the *Treaty Establishing a Constitution for Europe* (European Union 2004) ratified in 2004. Writers of that legal text chose not to cite European religious identity and rather mention other principles such as the rule of law. However, much of the discussion in the years of the drafting process of the *Constitution for Europe* revolved around the place of Christianity in the European identity (see Eriksen, Fossum and Menendez 2004), and this is how the civilizational perspective was present in that political debate.

In sum, Huntington criticized the structural realist paradigm by affirming the priority of culture over interest and power as the core of international politics, and by arguing that, in the new era, states were losing their centrality in favor of alliances and organizations based on shared civilizational values.

The Realist and Anti-Pelagian Character of Huntington's Thought

Even though the 'clash of civilizations' thesis is critical of some central tenets of structural realism, in this section, I argue that it shares some fundamental ideas with the classical realist tradition, which I have presented earlier in this chapter.

One of the objectives of Huntington's article and book on the 'clash of civilizations' is to advance arguments against other paradigms interpreting the post-Cold War world. In 1992, Francis Fukuyama's *The End of History,* among others, thought that the idea that the end of the Cold War was the beginning of an era without conflict. In this view, the world would have been united under one sole way of life and system of values: those inspired by liberal-democracy and by Western ideas. This conception is one of the many universalist political theories inspired by the idea of progress. Fukuyama was, as is well known, inspired by Hegel's philosophy and by Kojeve's Hegelian notion of 'universal homogeneous state', and considered the source of conflict to be ideological, or spiritual. Given the failure of all systems of ideas alternative to liberalism, history had reached its end (Fukuyama 2006). Another version of this view is represented by cosmopolitan theories of international politics according to which boundaries and particularist allegiances are morally irrelevant. From the increasing economic cooperation among states, communities and individuals follows the existence of a universal society in which burdens and benefits should be distributed and in which there are indeed universal human rights that are valid, beyond, and in spite of, all government bodies and legal recognitions of them (Pogge 2007, 2).

The paradigm advanced by Huntington is opposed to this optimist vision of world politics and advances objection to the view that conflict can be overcome. In general, the very idea of a world in which there is a plurality of civilizations is opposed to the notion that there is one and only one human civilization. There are indeed some elements common to all humans: 'certain basic values' and 'institutions' (2002, 6). However, Huntington argues, history can rather be explained in the light of the divisions among humanity, such as 'tribes, nations, and broader cultural entities normally called civilizations' (Huntington 2002, 56). Not only is a universal civilization based on Western values impossible, but the instauration of a global democracy is also doomed to failure (Huntington 2002, 193). Liberal universalist projects are, after all, imperialist and overlook cultural differences in the world. There is an irreducible cultural pluralism in the world, an irresolvable disagreement on fundamental values. There is no *lingua franca* among civilizations, and democracy and human rights are meaningful to the West but not to the rest. Huntington underlined the elements that separate human beings, and the importance of an 'us' versus 'them' logic in our quest for an identity. As he writes: 'people define their identity by what they are not' (Huntington 2002, 67).

What is important is that these differences are also the source of conflict and the reason world unity remains impossible. Instead of seeing history as a history of progress, with a bright future in which culture merges and peace advances, Huntington sees world politics as determined by the omnipresence of conflict. As in other realist writers, at the ground of this understanding there is a negative vision of human nature. As Huntington writes,

It is human to hate. For self-definition and motivation people need enemies: competitors in business, rivals in achievement, opponents in politics. They naturally distrust and see as threats those who are different and have the capability to harm them. The resolution of one conflict and the disappearance of one enemy generate personal, social, and political forces that give rise to new ones. The 'us' versus 'them' tendency is ... in the political arena almost universal. In the contemporary world the 'them' is more and more likely to be people from a different civilization (Huntington 2002, 130).

As many other European and American intellectuals before him, this negative view of humanity is paired with a certain reading of world history, in which the cultural force of the West is declining. The world of the clash of civilization is a world seen from a declining and ageing civilization that has lost control and appeal. This decline is in territory and population, economic product, military capability, but also cultural dominance (Huntington 2002, 83–96). As is well known and as many advocates of Huntington's ideas have suggested after 9/11 and after the recent terrorist attacks in Europe and America, the decline of the West is not leading the world to greater peace. Even though Huntington does not believe that a coalition of states against the West is possible (Huntington 2002, 185), civilizational relationships are antagonistic and conflict has to be considered the *leitmotiv* of international politics.

Conclusion

Huntington developed his paradigm of the 'clash of civilizations' in an age of turmoil and to answer the practical need of a new theory for the understanding of the world. The fall of the Soviet Union was the end of a (short) century of ideological and material wars between two systems of power. Likewise, the events that followed 9/11 also required a new vocabulary and a new way of interpreting the world. From the analysis conducted in this chapter it has emerged that Huntington found this vocabulary in the classical realist tradition. Even though Huntington was deeply critical of some of the assumptions of structural realism on the sources of conflict and on the role of states in international politics, he shared with the realists some important ideas. He grounds his views on an anti-utopian attitude, which dismisses all visions of world peace, inter-civilizational dialogue, cosmopolitan society, and universal civilization. Conflict, and the division of the world between friends and foes, is considered the essence of world politics, and even human nature.

References

Adib-Moghaddam, Arshin. 2010. *A Metahistory of the Clash of Civilizations.* London: Hurst & Company.

Boucher, David. 1998. Political Theories of International Relations. Oxford: Oxford University Press.

Eriksen, Erik Oddva, and John Erik Fossum, Agustín Menéndez. 2004. *Developing a Constitution for Europe.* London: Routledge.

European Union. 2004. *Treaty Establishing a Constitution for Europe*, 16 December, Official Journal of the European Union, C310, 16 December, available at: https://europa.eu/european.../treaty_establishing_a_constitution_for_europe_en.pdf Accessed 25 November 2017.

Fallaci, Oriana. 2002. *The Rage and the Pride.* Milano: Rizzoli.

Foucault, Michel. 2003. *Society Must Be Defended. Lectures at the Collège de France.* New York: Picador.

Fukuyama, Francis. 2006. *The End of History and the Last Man.* New York: Free Press.

Lebow, Richard Ned. 2003. *The Tragic Vision of Politics: Ethics, Interests, and Order.* Cambridge: Cambridge University Press.

Huntington, Samuel P. 1993. "The Clash of Civilizations?." *Foreign Affairs* 72, no. 3 (Summer): 22–49.

Huntington, Samuel P. 2002. *The Clash of Civilizations and the Remaking of World Order.* London: The Free Press.

Machiavelli, Niccolò. 1988. *The Prince.* Edited by Quentin Skinner and Russell Price. Cambridge: Cambridge University Press.

Mearsheimer, John. 2013. "Structural Realism." In *International Relations Theories: Discipline and Diversity,* 3rd Edition, edited by Tim Dunne, Milja Kurki, and Steve Smith, 77–93. Oxford: Oxford University Press.

Morgenthau, Hans J. 1948. *Politics Among Nations: The Struggle for Power and Peace.* 7th edition. New York: McGraw-Hill.

Morgenthau, Hans J, 1955. "Reflections on the State of Political Science." *The Review of Politics* 17(4): 431–60.

Oakeshott, Michael. 1991. *Rationalism in Politics and Other Essays.* Indianapolis: Liberty Fund.

Orsi, Davide, Janja R. Avgustin and Max Nurnus, eds. 2018. *Realism in Practice: An Appraisal.* Bristol: E-International Relations.

Pogge, Thomas. 2007. *Freedom from Poverty as a Human Right. Who Owes What to the Very Poor?.* Oxford: Oxford University Press.

Rengger, Nicholas. 2017. *The Anti-Pelagian Imagination in Political Theory and International Relations.* London: Routledge.

Rösch, Felix, and Richard Ned Lebow. 2017. "A Contemporary Perspective on Realism." In *International Relations Theory,* edited by Stephen McGlinchey, Rosie Walters and Christian Scheinpflug, 138–44. Bristol: E-International Relations.

Said, Edward. 2001. "The Clash of Ignorance." *The Nation,* 4 October. https://www.thenation.com/article/clash-ignorance/ Accessed 25 November 2017.

Schmitt, Carl. 2008. *The Concept of the Political.* Chicago: Chicago University Press.

Wight, Martin. 1966. "Why There is No International Theory." In *Diplomatic Investigations: Essays in the Theory of International Relations,* edited by Herbert Butterfield, Martin Wight, Hedley Bull, 17–34. London: Allen & Unwin.

2

Clashing Civilizations: A Toynbeean Response to Huntington

IAN HALL

Exactly forty years before *Foreign Affairs* published Samuel P. Huntington's original 'The Clash of Civilizations' article, in the northern summer of 1993, the British historian Arnold J. Toynbee was in the middle of a stormy debate about an equally controversial work of civilizational history and geopolitical prediction, *The World and the West* (Toynbee 1953). Three years away from retirement from his post at the Royal Institute of International Affairs (Chatham House), Toynbee was then 64 years old, and stood, as Huntington did in the early 1990s, at the pinnacle of his career, feted as modern sage for his sweeping grand historical studies and his acute analyses of international politics. His books were selling in the hundreds of thousands and his opinions on a wide range of topics avidly sought by the public (see McNeill 1989).[1]

The appearance of *The World and the West*, however, marked the start of Toynbee's fall from grace. Thereafter, his reputation began to decline, in part because the political views he expressed in that book – best thought of as left-liberal, internationalist, anti-colonial, and empathetic (though not sympathetic) towards Soviet Communism – were growing increasingly unfashionable, as Britain tried to reassert its grip on what remained of its empire and the Cold War-polarized political debate on both sides of the Atlantic (Hall 2012). In this context, Toynbee's argument in *The World and the West* and other publications that the West was 'the arch-aggressor of modern

---

[1]   On Toynbee's moment of 'Fame and Fortune', see McNeill 1989, 205–234. Toynbee's image even appeared on the cover of *Time* magazine, on 17 March 1947, with the title, referring to his prognostications about the West: 'Our civilization is not inexorably doomed'.

times' was not at all well received (Toynbee 1953, 2).[2] In parallel, his standing as a scholar fell too, as the historical profession grew much less tolerant of civilizational history, as well as the kind of religiosity Toynbee increasingly professed. Ironically, just as the idea of the 'West' became prominent in American and Western European political discourse, the concept of civilization was in the process of being set aside by academic historians as unhelpfully vague and imprecise (see Geyl 1956).

By the time Huntington revived 'civilization' as a unit of historical and geopolitical analysis in 1993, Toynbee's work had long been set aside as little more than a curiosity.[3] It is not surprising, therefore, that his ideas did not feature in Huntington's original *Foreign Affairs* article, nor that they received relatively short shrift in the book-length version of *The Clash of Civilizations* (Huntington 1993; Huntington 1998). But there are good reasons, I argue in what follows, to revisit Toynbee when reading Huntington's argument. His concept of civilization, developed in *A Study of History* (12 volumes, 1934–61), and especially his explorations of 'encounters' between civilizations and the effects he thought those encounters had, are useful instruments for destabilizing some of Huntington's key claims.

Defining Civilizations

There are many differences between Huntington and Toynbee's projects, especially in their conclusions and their policy prescriptions, but they had similar aims and assumptions. Both sought to use civilizational history to explain contemporary phenomena. Huntington's aim was to try to provide a parsimonious explanation for what he perceived as new patterns of behavior by states (and some non-state actors) in post-Cold War international relations, patterns that he argued could not adequately be explained by existing state-centric theories (Huntington 1998, 19–39). In particular, he was interested in the agitation and civil conflict that had emerged towards the end of the 1980s in parts of the Muslim world, in the soon-to-be-dissolved Soviet Union and state of Yugoslavia, between Hindu nationalists and Muslims in India, and between Tibetans and Han Chinese (Huntington 1993). Toynbee too was interested in explaining the causes of conflict, but his objective was to explain why the West had so catastrophically descended into a devastating war in 1914 and why international disorder persisted after 1919. Struck at the outset of the First World War by the apparent parallels between what he knew of ancient Greek history, especially of the Peloponnesian War, and the

---

[2]   For one vehement rebuttal, see Jerrold 1954. For a more measured assessment, see Perry 1982.

[3]   McNeill (1989, 243–258) traces this decline. Recently, there has been a mini-revival of Toynbee studies. See, for example, Hutton 2014 and Castellin 2015.

present, he set out to ascertain whether other past civilizations had experienced similar episodes of conflict – 'Times of Troubles', as he called them – and to determine whether the episodes had similar causes (Toynbee 1956b, 8; see also Hall 2014).

Both Huntington and Toynbee determined that the best way to explain the causes of contemporary conflicts was to look at civilizations rather than at states or other kinds of political or social groups. Toynbee began to explore this possibility first in *The Western Question in Greece and Turkey* (1922), which tried to explain the ferocity of the Greco-Turkish war of 1919–22, with its grim episodes of what later became known as ethnic-cleansing,[4] but only set it out in full in the first volume of his *Study of History* (1934). His argument was that historians must take a civilizational view of the past, because the histories of lesser social bodies made little sense in isolation. Civilizations, on this view, were the necessary context within which historical events must be interpreted, rather than things like nation-states, which were modern inventions (Toynbee 1934, 44–50). Huntington's account of a civilization was strikingly similar. In the book version of *The Clash of Civilizations* he defined a civilization as 'the broadest cultural entity' and argued that 'none of their constituent units can be fully understood without reference to the encompassing civilization' (Huntington 1998, 43 and 42). For both, only a civilizational view was sufficient to explain the phenomena they wanted to analyze.

Contacts and Clashes

Both Toynbee and Huntington acknowledged, of course, that these understandings of civilizations generated problems for the stories that they wanted to tell. Toynbee knew from the start that using a civilization to frame the interpretation of some historical episode might not, in fact, be sufficient. Civilizational boundaries (in so far as we can define them) are porous; civilizations interacted with others, and thus it might be necessary for historians to place things in an even wider context if they were to explain them properly. He had done this in the *Western Question*, a study of what happened when two civilizations came into contact 'in space', to use his language, but he had also long been concerned with contacts 'in time', where a civilization drew up inherited knowledge or beliefs from an earlier one.[5] In particular, as a classicist, Toynbee was interested in contacts between the ancient Greek or 'Hellenic' civilization, which he considered 'dead', and later civilizations, especially the transmission and mediation to the West of ideas

---

4   For background, see Clogg 1986.
5   The issue of contacts was the subject of Toynbee's (1954) *A Study of History*, vol. VIII.

and practices by the medieval Byzantine empire, but also the influence of the Hellenic ideas on both the Muslim and Hindu worlds.[6]

What Toynbee found in his *Study of History*, indeed, was that civilizations are rarely immune from outside influence, either from past civilizations or present ones. Only a couple of examples rose and fell in relative isolation, unaffected by others. Most emerged either out of a pre-existing civilization, drawing on its legacy of ideas and beliefs in a process Toynbee called, in his peculiar idiom, 'Apparentation-and-Affiliation'(1934, 97–105). Thus the West and the Orthodox world drew on Hellenic civilization; what he called the Babylonian and Hittite civilizations drew on the Sumerian; the two branches of the modern Islamic world, Arabic (Sunni) and 'Iranic' (Shia), drew on the pre-Islamic 'Syriac' civilization; and what he took to be contemporary 'Far Eastern' civilization, in China, Korea, and Japan, drew on a pre-existing but distinct 'Sinic' civilization, and so on (Toynbee 1954b, 107).[7] Then there were encounters between 'living' civilizations that shaped those involved. Some led to 'fruitful' exchanges (Toynbee gave the examples of the influence of Hellenic thought and art on ancient India, and then later on both medieval Christianity and Islam, as well as the Renaissance); some to the near total collapse of civilizations (such as those in the Americas); and some to retrenchment and resistance (as occurred in parts of the 'Far East' and the Muslim world when they encountered the modern West) (Toynbee 1954b).

Huntington, for his part, also wrestled in *The Clash of Civilizations* with the issue of boundaries and inter-civilizational contacts. He conceded that:

> Civilizations have no clear-cut boundaries and no precise beginnings and endings. People can and do redefine their identities and, as a result, the composition and shapes of civilizations change over time. The cultures of peoples interact and overlap.

He recognized too that civilizations 'evolve', observing that '[t]hey are dynamic, they rise and fall, they merge and divide' (Huntington 1998, 44). But Huntington insisted that '[c]ivilizations are nonetheless meaningful entities, and while the lines between them are seldom sharp, they are real' (Huntington 1998, 43). Moreover, he asserted that, historically, civilizations

---

[6]   For an early essay on this topic, see Toynbee 1923. In the essay, Toynbee wrote: 'Ancient Greek society perished at least as long ago as the seventh century A. D.', but that the West was its 'child' (289), the inheritor of a 'legacy bequeathed' (290). He recognized, however, that the Muslim and Hindu worlds were also heirs.

[7]   Some of these supposed civilizations, such as the 'Syriac', 'Sinic', and 'Far Eastern' were (and remain) controversial.

had rarely interacted, and there were few instances of inter-civilizational contact that led to really significant changes in the one or the other, until the modern era. Prior to 1500 CE, he argued, contacts between them were either 'nonexistent or limited' or 'intermittent and intense' (Huntington 1998, 48). Distance and transport technologies prevented anything more.

Only after 1500 CE, with the invention of new technologies that permitted more people to travel longer distances, Huntington maintained, did situations arise in which civilizations could be substantially changed by encounters with others. Importantly, however, he asserted that not all civilizations were changed to the same extent, and implied that some elements of a civilization – its cultural or religious kernel – could not be changed, though it could be destroyed. Instead, in the modern period, he argued '[i]ntermittent or limited multidirectional encounters among civilizations gave way to the sustained, overpowering, unidirectional impact of the West on all other civilizations' (Huntington 1998, 50). The result was the 'subordination of other societies to Western civilization'. This occurred not because of the superiority of Western ideas, Huntington insisted, but because of the superiority of Western technology, especially its military technology (Huntington 1998, 51). And despite their 'subordination' to Western power, he maintained, non-Western societies remained culturally distinct and resistant to Western cultural influence.

The technological unification of the world by the West thus brought into being, for Huntington, a 'multicivilizational system' characterized by 'intense, sustained, and multidirectional interactions among all civilizations' (Huntington 1998, 51). It had not, he went to great pains to argue, generated anything like a 'universal civilization'.[8] No universal language is in the process of formation, he argued; rather, languages once marginalized by imperial powers are being revived. Nor are we seeing a universal religion emerge; instead, adherents of major religions are becoming more entrenched in their beliefs, some even more fundamentalist. In sum, modernization has taken place without Westernization, strengthening non-Western cultures insofar as they have acquired new technologies, including new weapons, and reducing 'the relative power of the West' (Huntington 1998, 78).

Technologies and Ideas

Toynbee was also deeply concerned by the impact of the West on the rest of the world – that was the central theme of his incendiary *The World and the West*. His work on Turkey, during the First World War and after, left him well

---

[8]   Huntington devoted an entire chapter of the book to the debunking of that suggestion (1998, 56–78).

versed in the dynamics of modernization in a non-Western society, under the Ottomans and then under Kemal Ataturk. In his *Study of History* he ranged much further, examining Peter the Great and then the Bolshevik attempts to modernize Russia, the Meiji Restoration in Japan, and Sun Yat-sen's attempt to reform post-Qing China. He recognized that the spread of Western technologies to other societies was undercutting the relative power of the West, but he also emphasized that modern weapons and military science were not the only inventions that were aiding the revival of non-Western societies. Political and other ideas, including philosophical arguments and religious beliefs, Toynbee argued, had also changed those societies, and fueling what became known, in the 1950s, as the 'Revolt against the West' (Hall 2011).

Although during the course of writing *A Study of History*, Toynbee offered different accounts of what occurred when civilizations encountered each other, he was consistent in insisting that the effects were much more dramatic than Huntington suggested. Like Edward Gibbon, he argued that 'major' religions were the product of the intrusion of 'foreign' ideas into a civilization, as Christianity had arisen as Jewish millenarianism, appeared on the fringes of the Greco-Roman world, slowly infected its consciousness and – for the young Toynbee as for Gibbon – destroyed that classical world (Gibbon 2010). Later, as Toynbee shed his liberal rationalist agnosticism and became more sympathetic to religion, his view of the birth of Christianity and other major religions changed (see Toynbee 1956a), but he remained convinced that ideas transmitted by inter-civilizational encounters could bring about major social and political changes within civilizations. Like Huntington, he argued that encounters might lead to the transmission of just one technology or idea and not others, much less to an entire corpus of civilizational ideas and beliefs. In *The World and the West*, as we have seen, he detailed how modern technology had been transmitted to Russia, Turkey, and the 'Far East', while Western religious ideas, for example, had been rejected. Toynbee suggested we understand this process by way of a metaphor borrowed from physics. This was what happened, he argued, 'when the culture-ray of a radioactive civilization hits a foreign body social', as the latter's 'resistance diffracts the culture-ray into its component strands' (Toynbee 1953, 67).

Toynbee rightly recognized, however, that modern military technology was not the only thing that had been transmitted to the non-West during the period of Western imperial expansion. He was particularly concerned with the transmission of political ideas, especially nationalism and the concept of the nation-state, 'an exotic institution', as he put it, 'deliberately imported from the West...simply because the West's political power had given the West's political institutions an irrational yet irresistible prestige in non-Western eyes' (Toynbee 1953, 71). A sound internationalist, Toynbee was deeply exercised by this spread of nationalism and the nation-state, an institution he thought both obsolete, given the economic unification of the world, and even more worryingly, prone to being set up as some kind of false idol for the masses to worship (Toynbee 1956a, 27–36).[9] But setting this normative spin aside, his core point – that inter-civilizational encounters spread more than technology and weapons – is surely irrefutable; indeed, the notion that the sovereign state, organized along national lines or not, was spread by Western imperial expansions is the consensus view in contemporary International Relations (see Bull and Watson 1984).

Toynbee was deeply troubled also by the spread of things like Western consumerism, which he thought, like Mohandas Gandhi, could even infect non-Western societies like India to their detriment (Toynbee 1953, 79–80). But at the same time, he outlined a more positive message, which also challenges key elements of Huntington's thesis, and sits uneasily with other aspects of his own thinking. Although much of Toynbee's *Study of History* was taken up by warnings against mimesis or the imitation of others, as well as pleas for authentic creative 'responses' to 'challenges',[10] he was also convinced that the technological and economic unification of the world by the West had fundamentally changed our – humanity's – historical perspective.

This change generated a number of effects. First, Toynbee observed, it made it harder for certain societies to think of themselves as a 'Chosen People' and uniquely civilized (Toynbee 1948, 71–79). A few in the postwar West, he thought, still suffered from this delusion, but it would pass in time, as they realized that Western history was not as unique as they had been taught (Toynbee 1948, 79). Second, it was now possible to study the thought of others' civilizations. Non-Westerners, he noted, were doing this in numbers, 'taking Western lessons at first-hand in the universities of Paris or Cambridge and Oxford; at Columbia and at Chicago', as was right and proper as the heirs to the riches of all past and contemporary civilizations. Some had 'caught...the Western ideological disease of Nationalism', Toynbee lamented, but at least their historical perspective was no longer 'parochial' (Toynbee 1948, 83). They, he observed, 'have grasped the fact that...*our* past history has become a vital part of *theirs* [italics in original]'. What was needed was for Westerners to make a similar leap, recognizing that Africa's or China's past was also 'theirs', in the same way that they regard the histories of the 'extinct civilizations' of 'Israel, Greece and Rome' as theirs (Toynbee 1948, 89).

---

[9]   He also warned against the idolatrous worship of world-states, philosophers, religious institutions, and technology, among other things.

[10]   See especially Toynbee, *Study of History*, vols. II and III. Creative responses to challenges, he posited, brought about 'growth' (that is, loosely, progress) in civilizations. He derived this theory from a number of sources, especially from the French philosopher Henri Bergson.

The unification of the world, Toynbee argued, meant that all histories belonged to all, and that meant the distinction between Western and non-Western was no longer tenable:

> Our own descendants are not going to be just Western, like ourselves. They are going to be heirs of Confucius and Lao-Tse [sic] as well as Socrates, Plato, and Plotinus; heirs of Gautama Buddha as well as Deutero-Isaiah and Jesus Christ; heirs of Zarathustra and Muhammed as well as Elijah…; heirs of Shankara and Ramanuja as well as Clement and Origen;… and heirs…of Lenin and Gandhi and Sun Yat-sen as well as Cromwell and George Washington and Mazzini (Toynbee 1948, 90).

This was heady stuff, of course, and it led Toynbee off toward trying to come up with a plan for a syncretic religion, blending insights from existing ones, that might serve to overcome political conflict and serve as the basis for the future reconciliation of the world (see Toynbee 1956a; Toynbee 1954a). But his core point – that the philosophies and concepts of all civilizations, both 'living' and 'extinct', were now for the first time available for all to read, study, adopt, and adapt, accepting the challenges of translation – was a powerful one, especially in view of Huntington's insistence that civilizations are divided along sharp lines, despite the economic and technological unification of the world.

Conclusion

The conclusion to the book version of *The Clash of Civilizations* opens, oddly enough, with a discussion of Toynbee's warning of the 'mirage of immortality' he thought beguiled and distracted civilizations in decline (Toynbee 1945a, 301). But where Toynbee called for an effort to draw upon the inheritance bequeathed by all civilizations to construct new social and political institutions befitting of the 'ecumenical community' created by the West's unification of the world (Toynbee 1954a), Huntington argued for something narrower . In *The Clash of Civilizations* and especially in *Who are We?* (2004), he called for the renewal and revival of the West, which he thought had been weakened by immigration and by multiculturalism, which aided and abetted the spread of non-Western cultural and religious beliefs and practices, by economic malaise, and by 'moral decay'(1998, 304). The United States, he argued, must defend the Anglo-Saxon Protestant beliefs and practices that delivered past social and political success, so as to ensure it can play the necessary role of the West's 'core state'.

Toynbee, of course, warned against such policies, which he characterized as anachronistic archaisms. But more importantly, as we have seen, his *Study of History* raises questions about the assumptions that underlie Huntington's prescriptions. In particular, Toynbee's work suggests that historical encounters between civilizations were more frequent and consequential than Huntington allowed. Second, it points to the extent of the transmission not just of technologies, but also of social and political ideas, and to their impact, as bodies of thought like Jewish millenarianism encountered Hellenic philosophy to create Christianity, for example, or indeed how Christian ideas shaped Hindu revivalism.[11] Third, it draws attention to agency and away from Huntington's overly structural account of ideas and beliefs, pointing to the role played by both scholars and political actors in borrowing, accepting, appropriating, and indeed manipulating 'foreign' philosophies and religious concepts, as well as technologies, for their own purposes, as Toynbee's non-Western students did when they recognized, implicitly or not, Western history as 'theirs' as well as 'ours'. In turn, of course, that draws attention to the great unanswered, pressing question of *The Clash of Civilizations*: who is responsible for this resurgence of cultural and religious politics in the post-Cold War era?

References

Bagby, Philip. 1959. *Culture and History: Prolegomena to the Comparative Study of Civilizations*. Berkeley: University of California Press.

Bull, Hedley and Adam Watson, eds. 1984. *The Expansion of International Society*. Oxford: Clarendon.

Castellin, Luca G. 2015. "Arnold J. Toynbee's Quest for a New World Order: A Survey." *The European Legacy* 20(6): 619–635.

Clogg, Richard. 1986. *Politics and the Academy: Arnold Toynbee and the Koraes Chair*. London: Frank Cass.

Geyl, Pieter. 1956. "Toynbee's System of Civilizations." In *Toynbee and History: Critical Essays and Reviews* edited by M. F. Ashley Montagu. Boston: Porter Sargent, 39–76.

Gibbon, Edward. 2010. *The Decline and Fall of the Roman Empire*, vols. I–VI. London: Everyman's.

---

[11]   On the impact of Christianity on, for instance, Swami Vivekananda's Hindu revivalism, see Sharma 2013.

Hall, Ian. 2011. "The Revolt against the West: Decolonization and its Repercussions in British International Thought, 1960–1985." *International History Review* 33(1): 43–64.

Hall, Ian. 2014. "'Time of Troubles': Arnold J. Toynbee's Twentieth Century." *International Affairs* 90(1): 23–36.

Hall, Ian. 2012. "'The Toynbee Convector': The Rise and Fall of Arnold J. Toynbee's Anti-Imperial Mission to the West." *The European Legacy* 17(4): 459–466.

Huntington, Samuel P. 1993. "The Clash of Civilizations?." *Foreign Affairs* 72(3): 31–35.

Huntington, Samuel P. 1998. *The Clash of Civilizations and the Remaking of World Order*. London: Touchstone.

Huntington, Samuel P. 2004. *Who are We? The Challenges to America's National Identity*. New York: Simon & Schuster.

Hutton, Alexander. 2014. "'A belated return for Christ?': The reception of Arnold J. Toynbee's *A Study of History* in a British context, 1934–1961." *European Review of History* 21(3): 405–424.

Jerrold, Douglas. (954. *The Lie about the West: A Response to Professor Toynbee's Challenge*. London: J. M. Dent.

McNeill, William H. 1989. *Arnold J. Toynbee: A Life*. New York: Oxford University Press.

Melko, Matthew. 1969. *The Nature of Civilizations*. Boston: Porter Sargent.

Perry, Marvin. 1982. *Arnold Toynbee and the Crisis of the West*. Washington, DC: University Press of America.

Sharma, Jyotirmaya. 2013. *A Restatement of Religion: Swami Vivekananda and the Making of Hindu Nationalism*. New Haven: Yale University Press.

Toynbee, Arnold J. 1922. *The Western Question in Greece and Turkey: A Study in the Contact of Civilizations*. London: Constable.

Toynbee, Arnold J. 1923. "History." In *The Legacy of Greece* edited by R. W. Livingstone, 289–290. Oxford: Clarendon.

Toynbee, Arnold J. 1934. *A Study of History*, vol. I. London: Oxford University Press.

Toynbee, Arnold J. 1948. *Civilization on Trial*. New York: Oxford University Press.

Toynbee, Arnold J.1953. *The World and the West*. New York: Oxford University Press.

Toynbee, Arnold J. 1954a. *A Study of History*, vol. VII. London: Oxford University Press.

Toynbee, Arnold J. 1954b. *A Study of History*, vol. VIII. London: Oxford University Press.

Toynbee, Arnold J. 1956a. *An Historian's Approach to Religion*. London: Oxford University Press.

Toynbee, Arnold J. 1956b. "A Study of History – What the Book is for: How the Book Took Shape." In *Toynbee and History: Critical Essays and Reviews* edited by M. F. Ashley Montagu. Boston: Porter Sargent, 8–11.

Voegelin, Eric. 1956–87. *Order and History*, vols. I–V. Baton Rouge: Louisiana State University Press.

3

Samuel Huntington and the American Way of War

ERIK RINGMAR

It is now 25 years ago that Samuel Huntington published his 'Clash of Civilizations' article in *Foreign Affairs* (Huntington 1993). In the time that has passed since then it has become abundantly clear why his argument fails. Understood as an explanation of the logic of world politics, his thesis is simply untenable. 'This book is not intended', as he admitted in the longer version of the argument, 'to be a work of social science' (Huntington 1996, 13). There is in fact nothing much that Huntington can either explain or predict. His discussion of the various 'civilizations' and their supposed features remind you of a textbook from a Chinese middle-school with its portrayal of 'the five races of mankind and their inherent characteristics'. None of this can be taken seriously. Moreover, the argument is offensive. It is offensive to be boxed into a 'civilization' and to be told that you are the same as the people confined to the same box, and that, moreover, you are sufficiently different from the people confined to other boxes for there to be confrontations between you. Well, many of us would not like to be put in the same box as Huntington. It is enough to make you want to go put on a hijab.

If, on the other hand, all Huntington ever wanted to say was that 'culture' matters, he is not saying anything original or new. Only the most doctrinaire of Neorealists ever believed that ideas play no role in world politics. The Cold War, colonialism, Putin in the Crimea, the European Union, economic development and trade, migration and global warming – it is all a matter of ideas and values; that is, a matter of culture. But the rest of us knew that already and we did not need 9/11 to remind us.

In this article we will do three things. First we will draw a distinction between 'cultures' and 'civilizations' and explain why civilizations cannot clash.

Secondly, we will make use of a historical example – the Second Opium War, 1856–1860 – in order to explain how 'civilizational wars' come about. Finally, we will reflect on the place of such wars in American foreign policy and on Huntington's own role in fomenting civilizational conflicts.

Why Civilizations Cannot Clash

'Clash', says the dictionary, is a word of onomatopoeic origin with three basic definitions ('Clash' 2017). The first meaning, closest to the sound made by the word itself, is the 'din resulting from two or more things colliding'. The second meaning is 'skirmish' or 'hostile encounter', no doubt derived from the sound two swords make as they engage. The third meaning denotes an opposition or a contradiction of some kind, such as 'a clash of beliefs' or personalities. Garments too can clash if, for example, their colors do not match. It is as if the beliefs, personalities or garments, synesthetically, made a din. Yet civilizations cannot clash, we will argue, since they are not the kinds of things which, synesthetically or otherwise, make a din when juxtaposed.

In order to see why, let us continue our etymological exposé. Compare 'cultures' with 'civilizations'. Culture refers to 'cultivation', that is, to the 'tilling of the land' ('Culture' 2017). To cultivate a plant is to care for it and to make it grow. Metaphorically speaking, what is being cultivated by a culture is the human soul – compare individuals and societies that 'flourish', 'flower' or 'bloom'. What grows always grows in a particular location and farmers are sedentary since they must stay in one place to plant the crop, water and weed it, to harvest and store it. In order to protect what we grow, we drive stakes into the ground and build fences which separate what is ours from that which belongs to others. Engaged in these activities, we make a place out of space. These few acres are the land that feeds us, which fed our ancestors and which will feed our descendants in turn. Cultures, we believe, can be nurtured and protected in the same fashion. A culture is always *our* culture, it belongs to people like us, the place where we live, and it identifies who we are. The solid walls that surround it safeguard our way of life and keep trespassers out.

If culture finds its metaphorical basis in agriculture, civilization finds it in exchange. A *civis* is a 'citizen', a city-dweller, and as such he or she is 'civilized' in a way that peasants never can be. City people, they will themselves tell us, are not country bumpkins. They get their food from shops, not from the ground; they have clean hands and clean clothes; they drive sports cars and drink café lattes. And while city-dwellers typically consider this level of sophistication to be a result of their personal achievements, it is really a consequence of the exchange networks to which cities are connected. It is these networks – including places located very far away indeed – that civilize them. Through the networks we come into contact with things that can be compared and judged in relation to each other, and suddenly we have a choice between better and cheaper options, between the newer and the never-before-tried. This broadens our horizons and improves our lives. This is why civilization depends on the unencumbered circulation of goods, people, ideas, faiths and ways of life. Thus while cultures require walls, civilizations require bridges. As a result, in cities we always come across unexpected things and strange people. The effect may be unsettling but also liberating. We no longer have to be confined to, and carry the burden of, our culture; we no longer have to be who we are. Civilization provides us with a means of escape. *Stadtluft macht frei.*

This is not Huntington's definition of a civilization to be sure. To Huntington a civilization is 'the highest cultural grouping of people and the broadest level of cultural identity people have short of that which distinguishes humans from other species' (Huntington 1993, 24). Civilization, that is, is a sort of super- or perhaps supra-culture. For us, by contrast, a civilization has no particular content but denotes instead a mechanism or a social practice. Civilization is a process – a *civilizing process* – which works by means of openness and exchange. Civilization, for that reason, has no particular content but operates instead with whatever cultural content the historical context provides. Take the Muslims in *al-Andalus*. They civilized Spain in the ninth century by connecting its cities to the great centers of Arabic culture in the Middle East. In fact, they connected Spain to Persian culture too, and to Indian, Central Asia, and even Chinese. As a result of these civilizing connections, the great library in Córdoba had books made of paper, not vellum, and was far larger than any library in Christian Europe; the old Visigoths came to eat lemons, play the lute and compose far better poetry; they used better plows and irrigation techniques too, and put on deodorant and brushed their teeth with toothpaste. Or consider how the entire canon of classical Greek texts, saved for posterity by the caliphs of Baghdad, was transmitted to Spain where the works of Aristotle, Hippocrates and Ptolemy for the first time became available in Latin. Europeans later came to call this 'the Renaissance'.

Islam, Huntington claimed in a statement endlessly recycled after 9/11, 'has bloody borders' (Huntington 1993, 35). This is not the case, not because Muslims are nicer than Huntington gave them credit for, but because civilizations have no borders. Borderlessness, we said, is a defining characteristic of a civilizing process. This, indeed, is why the word 'civilization' was put within scare quotes by German authors in the nineteenth century (Spengler 1927). To them, civilization was a superficial idea, something which anyone could pick up in the market place, or something, like a shirt, which you easily can change and discard. A *Kultur*, by contrast, is the very skin that contains your body; it defines who you are and cannot be exchanged or thrown away. The Germans of the nineteenth century loved their *Kultur* not because it necessarily was better than other cultures but simply because it was theirs. This was the problem with the *liberté, égalité, fraternité* of the French Revolution. Once slogans like these began spreading across Europe, they were not confined to a specific society and belonged to no one in particular. They had a universal reach – compare the *Déclaration des droits de l'homme* of 1789 – designed to appeal to the largest number of customers. There was nothing wrong with these catchphrases, but they corresponded to no lived reality.

Strictly speaking, and we are speaking strictly here, cultures cannot clash. Cultures simply exist side by side, each one rooted to its own particular soil. The fences and the walls separating them make sure that there is no mixing and no miscegenation. From this point of view a 'culture clash' is something that occurs because a person from a society with one culture moves to a society with another culture. The cultures are not moving, people are. The din of the clashes ceases when the person finally has come to adjust to the new conditions. When in Nome, we do like the nomads.

But civilizations cannot clash either. Exchange is an activity in which you engage freely; it is an affair between consenting adults. Exchange is all a matter of how much something costs per kilo; how many pennies for your thoughts; how many tits for a tat. And you can always refuse to make a deal. Free trade, by definition, cannot be forced (Ringmar 2011a). Markets for that reason operate as a conflict resolving device. Instead of making a big, centralized, decision which people end up fighting over, the conflict can be resolved if you turn it into a myriad of small, decentralized, decisions which individuals make for themselves. Since the civilizing process operates by means of such self-regulation, civilizations do not clash.

The problem, however, is that civilizations can come to clash with cultures and cultures with civilizations. The lived reality, to speak with the nineteenth-century Germans, can come to be exchanged for the superficial catchphrase; a person's real face for a mask; the skin for a shirt – and this, unsurprisingly, can be a cause for concern and resentment. This is how civilizational wars happen.

Why 'Civilizational Wars' Happen

The nineteenth century was an era of colonial warfare; it was also an era of 'civilizational wars,' or what we really should call 'a clash between two cultures occasioned by a process of exchange.' The French had a *mission civilisatrice* which took their soldiers and colonial administrators from the mountains of Kabylia to the jungles of Vietnam. Meanwhile, the British shouldered the 'white man's burden' in India, in Africa, and in most other corners of the globe. The Germans, for their part, did their best to improve the lives of the indigenous population of southwestern Africa (Erichsen and Olusoga 2010). The savages must be civilized, even if it goes against their will; failing that, we must control them, and failing that, *alas*, the savages might have to be killed. And the wars intended to spread European culture have continued to this day, although we might refer to them as 'promoting democracy' or 'freedom', or perhaps as a 'duty to protect'.

Importantly, in the background of these conflicts are the culture-transforming forces unleashed by the rapid expansion of global markets in the nineteenth century. No one has written about this better than Karl Marx and Friedrich Engels. It is the 'profit motive', they argued in *The Communist Manifesto*, which set the Europeans on a chase for markets around the world (Marx and Engels 1910 [1848]). And once the search for profits came to replace all other concerns, each culture was dramatically transformed. The profit motive destroyed feudal relations and replaced them with market relations; it shook up old habits, confounded established truths and toppled old gods. Culture was everywhere replaced by civilization. The profit motive 'compels all nations, on the pain of extinction, to adopt the bourgeois mode of production; it compels them to introduce what it calls civilization into their midst, *i.e.*, to become bourgeois themselves' (Marx and Engels 1910 [1848], 18).

The great example which Marx and Engels had in mind was the opening up of China which was expected in the wake of the Treaty of Nanjing, concluded in 1842, six years before *The Communist Manifesto* was published. 'The cheap prices of commodities', as they put it, are the 'heavy artillery' which 'batters down all Chinese walls' (Marx and Engels 1910 [1848], 18). The British business community had long waited for such access. China contained, they believed, some 350 million eager consumers – 'a third of mankind' – and if they only could reach them, enormous profits were to be made. The problem was only that the Chinese authorities refused to open up – the only trade permitted took place with the one city ('Canton') of Guangzhou in the south. This was obviously not good enough and eventually the British merchants convinced their government to go to war with the Chinese over the issue – two wars, in fact, the two Opium Wars, 1839–42 and 1856–60. Marx and Engels were wrong, in other words. Cheap prices were *not* the 'heavy artillery' which forced the walls of China to come down. Instead the walls came down by means of the heavy artillery of heavy artillery.

To the British this was not only a commercial but a civilizational war. Hiding behind their walls the Chinese had become utterly ignorant of world affairs, the British argued; they knew nothing, for example, of the remarkable inventions and discoveries which recently had taken place in Europe. China was stagnant, ruled by 'the despotism of custom', and since the country never changed, it had no history (Mill 1849, 126–127; 130). At best the Chinese were 'half-civilized', but many Europeans considered them simply as 'barbarians'. If the country is to improve, John Stuart Mill argued in 1859, 'it must be by foreigners'. Fortunately, just such help was at hand. In October 1860, a combined Anglo-French army made it to Yuanmingyuan, a large compound of palaces and pleasure gardens located northwest of Beijing, which contained the emperor's vast collection of works of art, treasure, and a full-scale library (Ringmar 2013b; Ringmar 2011b, 273–98). First the French looted the palaces and then the British burned down the whole compound down. Some critics, the authorities back in London worried, might consider this an 'act of barbarism', but a measure of barbarism is required if we ever are to civilize the Chinese. Only a great jolt can awaken them from their stupor.

When news of the wars in China reached London, Lord Palmerston, the prime minister, was pleased. Palmerston was a liberal and a staunch defender of Britain's commercial interests abroad. In power almost continuously from the beginning of the nineteenth century, he never missed an opportunity to stress the civilizing impact of commerce. It would be 'to the great and manifest advantage of the people of China if a larger commercial intercourse were established between them and other countries' (Palmerston 1857, 1827). 'I am heartily glad', he wrote when the destruction of the Yuanmingyuan was completed. 'It was absolutely necessary to stamp by some such permanent record our indignation at the treachery and brutality of these Tartars' (Stanmore 1906, 350). 'These semi-barbarous Governments appear to deal with each other with treachery and cruelty', as he put it to parliament, 'and they are apt to think that they may act in the same manner against civilized Governments. It was, therefore, necessary to prove to them by some signal retribution that such deeds are not to be committed with impunity' (Palmerston 1843, 403–4).

Yet not everyone in England agreed (Ringmar 2011a, 5–32). Edward Smith Stanley, the 14th Earl of Derby, was a conservative critic. Derby was a Tory and a former prime minister, who was deeply suspicious of democracy but also of free trade. He had defended the protectionist Corn Laws back in the 1840s and he had no time for talk of 'civilizing missions'. Derby was proud of British liberties but believed they were rooted in British traditions and could not simply be dug up and exported abroad. It was his love of his own culture which made him respect the cultures of others. Now he defended the Chinese. 'I am an advocate', he began an hour-long speech to parliament, 'for perplexed and bewildered barbarism against the arrogant demands of overweening, self-styled civilization. I am an advocate for the feeble defenselessness of China against the overpowering might of Great Britain' (Derby 1857, 1155). Derby refused to accept that it had been necessary to destroy the imperial palaces. 'I think it likely to produce a painful and prejudicial impression against us as to the mode in which we carry on our military operations, and it appears to me to have been a mistake in point both of judgment and policy' (Derby 1861, 384).

Another critic was Richard Cobden. He was in all respects the very opposite of Derby: a radical and a self-made man, a founding member of the Anti-Corn Law League and the most vocal proponent of free trade both in and outside of parliament. Cobden believed in all the progressive causes of the day: a broadened franchise, abolition of the church rates, Catholic emancipation. He was active in the peace movement too and a supporter of disarmament and negotiated settlements of international conflicts. Cobden strongly supported the liberal values he associated with European civilization, but he was at the same time adamant that civilization cannot be spread by violent means. It is only through the power of our example that we can convince the Chinese to open their borders. Meanwhile, said Cobden, China deserves our respect: 'If in speaking of them we stigmatize them as barbarians, and threaten them with force because we say they are inaccessible to reason, it must be because we do not understand them; because their ways are not our ways, nor our ways theirs' (Cobden 1857, 1420–21).

Cultures cannot clash, we said, and neither can civilizations, but civilizations can clash with cultures and cultures with civilizations. Modeling our explanation on the example provided by the Opium Wars, we can conclude that the first step to a 'civilizational war' – 'a clash between two cultures occasioned by a process of exchange' – is taken when the political representatives of a culture feel threatened by the impact of openness and free markets and decide to protect themselves against it. The second step is taken when the proponents of free exchange oppose such measures and decide to remove them by force. The problem, in other words, is not the conservatives – the Lord Derbys of this world – they are friendly, if deeply conservative, multiculturalists. Multiculturalists are happy to live and let live and they take it for granted that cultures can exist peacefully coexist side by side. Neither is the problem the true liberals – the likes of Richard Cobden. True liberals are peace-loving free-traders who insist that exchange must be free and who trust the civilizing process to run its course. The problem is rather the liberals with access to firearms and the determination to use them – Palmerston and his ilk in the nineteenth century and their armed, liberal, counterparts today. They are the ones who wage 'civilizational wars' by barbarian means; establish democracy and human rights at gunpoint, and impose free trade by force.

'Civilizational Wars' and US Foreign Policy

After 25 years, we said, we all know what the problem is with Samuel Huntington's 'Clash of Civilizations' thesis. It is bad social science, or rather no social science at all; it is as clichéd as a Chinese middle-school textbook; it is offensive since it forces people into boxes which are set in opposition to each other. Moreover, we can now add, it is dangerous and war-mongering. But in order to understand the danger which Huntington's argument represents we need to place it in the context of the American way of war.

Compare Europe. Wars in Europe from the early modern period onwards were fought between states that all resembled each other. Culturally European states were all more or less alike and what separated them was nothing but their respective *Staatsräson* and the logic of power politics. They were constantly at war with each other mainly since the anarchical logic of their international system made it impossible for one country to trust its neighbors and since the means devised to assure peace – balances of power and alliance politics – often proved insufficient. Europeans shared the same culture – what they, and later Huntington, called the same 'civilization' – and among civilized people, they argued, you could expect a certain kind of conduct. Civilized people are not supposed to kill unarmed prisoners of war, for example, to loot libraries and places of religious worship, or to destroy the foundations of ordinary people's livelihood. However, none of these rules applied in wars with people outside of Europe, and the reason was that the 'savages' the Europeans encountered here fought their wars by savage means (Ringmar 2013a). That is, they made no distinctions between soldiers and civilians, never hesitated to kill children or mothers or to destroy crops, orchards and animals (Colby 1927). In order to defeat such enemies, the Europeans concluded, they too had to become savages. Colonial warfare was for that reason extraordinarily brutal.

When Americans in the nineteenth century turned their backs on Europe, they turned their backs on the European type of wars. Only corrupt kings and their scheming advisers, the inhabitants of the New World decided, would quibble over *Staatsräson* and balances of power. The United States was to be a new and better kind of society, established in the wilderness of the new continent. Differently put, American society was constituted in relation to a frontier, the other side of which was inhabited by non-Europeans. The obvious question was how to relate to them. One alternative would have been Lord Derby's multi-cultural solution. Cultures, we said, do not have to clash, and American and native cultures could quite easily have lived peacefully side by side.

Another alternative would have been Cobden's pacific exchange. The natives were eager tradesmen, after all, and their societies were also quickly transformed under the impact of world markets. But none of this was to happen. The Americans were settlers, we should not forget; they were colonizers, and soon the frontiers of their empire expanded rapidly westward (Grant 1933). As a result, all the wars in which they engaged were wars fought on behalf of their way of life. And when the American landmass finally was exhausted, the civilizational wars continued in the Philippines, Vietnam, and more recently against 'savages' in Afghanistan and Iraq.

The Europeans fought wars on behalf of their culture too, we said, but the difference is that they took place in the colonies and the colonies were always very far away. As such the 'civilizational wars' came only to involve a small fringe of the population. Europeans in general did *not* follow colonial events and the colonies had *little* impact on popular conceptions of the world or on European society (Porter 2004). Returning home from the colonies, few people wanted to listen to the soldiers' stories and instead they were often criticized for the uncivilized ways in which they treated the natives. The colonial soldiers reacted with resentment and pointed to the hypocrisy of the people at home who wanted the goal but were not willing to agree to the means (Pontecorvo 1966). A gulf separated the *pieds noirs* from the general population and the former were generally considered by the latter as militaristic cranks. The Europeans still fight wars on behalf of their culture – the French intervention in Mali in 2013 is a recent example – but they are still wars of a colonial type that leave little impact on European society.

In America it did not work this way. The wars fought on behalf of American culture were not fought in some far-away colony but right at home. They did not concern the interests of a small fringe, but instead the very existence and survival of the country. The soldiers who returned home from the fronts were greeted as heroes and given prominent places in government; the *pieds noirs* were incorporated into the state. This established a tradition of thinking about oneself in relation to the rest of the world but also a certain American way of making war. It is simply inconceivable that someone with the mindset of a Rumsfeld, a Cheney, a Wolfowitz or a Perle would make it in European politics. In the U.S., by contrast, militaristic cranks such as these became members of the establishment. It is equally impossible, let us conclude, that someone with Samuel Huntington's mindset would make it in European academia. It is not that Europeans are from Venus and Americans from Mars; it is rather that Americans still are fighting the 'civilizational wars' of the nineteenth century. For the past 25 years, Huntington's thesis has aided and abetted liberals with access to firearms; presenting them with suggestions, imperatives and hopes. As such his argument is likely to produce just the kinds of wars it purports to explain. It is a classic self-fulfilling prophecy.

* I am grateful to Amanda Cheney, Diane Pranzo, Eric Sangar, Ted Svensson and an audience at Stance, Lund University, for comments and suggestions on a previous version.

References

"Clash." 2017. *Wiktionary*. https://en.wiktionary.org/wiki/clash Accessed 14 November 2017.

Cobden, Richard. 1857. "The War in China." *Hansard*, House of Commons, 144: 1391–1485.

Colby, Elbridge. 1927. "How to Fight Savage Tribes." *The American Journal of International Law* 21, no. 2 (April): 279–88.

"Culture." 2017. *Wiktionary*. https://en.wiktionary.org/wiki/culture Accessed 14 November 2017.

Derby, Edward Henry Stanley. 1861. "Vote of Thanks." *Hansard*, House of Lords 161: 366–93.

Derby, Edward Henry Stanley. 1857. "War with China." *Hansard*, House of Lords 144: 1155–1245.

Erichsen, Casper, and David Olusoga. 2010. *The Kaiser's Holocaust: Germany's Forgotten Genocide and the Colonial Roots of Nazism*. London: Faber & Faber, 2010.

Grant, Madison. 1993. *Conquest of a Continent: Or, The Expansion of Races in American*. New York: C. Scribner's sons.

Huntington, Samuel P. 1993. "The Clash of Civilizations?" *Foreign Affairs* 72(3): 22–49.

Huntington, Samuel P. 1996. *The Clash of Civilizations and the Remaking of World Order*. New York: Simon & Schuster.

Marx, Karl, and Friedrich Engels. 1910 [1848]. *Manifesto of the Communist Party*. Translated by Samuel Moore. Chicago: Charles H. Kerr & company.

Mill, John Stuart. 1859. *On Liberty*. London: John W. Parker & Son.

Palmerston, Third Viscount. 1843. "China: Vote of Thanks." *Hansard*, House of Commons, 66: 547–74.

Palmerston, Third Viscount. 1857. "The War in China." *Hansard*, House of Commons, 144: 1726–1846.

Pontecorvo, Gillo. 1966. *La battaglia di Algeri*. Rialto Pictures. Film.

Porter, Bernard. 2004. "'Empire, What Empire?': Or, Why 80% of Early-and Mid-Victorians Were Deliberately Kept in Ignorance of It." *Victorian Studies* 46(2): 256–63.

Ringmar, Erik. 2011a. "Free Trade by Force: Civilization against Culture in the Great China Debate of 1857." In *Culture and External Relations: Europe and Beyond*, edited by Jozef Bátora and Monika Mokre, 5–32. Aldershot: Ashgate.

Ringmar, Erik. 2011b. "Malice in Wonderland: Dreams of the Orient and the Destruction of the Palace of the Emperor of China." *Journal of World History* 22(2): 273–98.

Ringmar, Erik. 2013a. "'How to Fight Savage Tribes': The Global War on Terror in Historical Perspective." *Terrorism and Political Violence* 25(2): 264–83.

Ringmar, Erik. 2013b. *Liberal Barbarism: The European Destruction of the Palace of the Emperor of China*. New York: Palgrave.

Spengler, Oswald. 1927. *The Decline of the West: Form and Actuality*. Translated by Charles Francis Atkinson. New York: Alfred A. Knopf.

Stanmore, Arthur H. 1906. *Sidney Herbert, Lord Herbert of Lea: A Memoir*. London: Murray

4

Why (Clash of) Civilizations Discourses Just Won't Go Away? Understanding the Civilizational Politics of Our Times

GREGORIO BETTIZA & FABIO PETITO

The notion that relations between civilizations are central drivers of international politics has become a key feature of international relations discourses and practices since the end of the Cold War. Some see these relations as marked by conflict and confrontation, most notably in the case of Samuel Huntington's (1996, 1993) 'Clash of Civilizations' theory. Similar ideas, however, can also be found in Bernard Lewis' (2002) analysis of the malaise afflicting the Muslim world, in the 'Asian values' debate (Zakaria and Yew 1994), or in Aleksandr Dugin's (2014) efforts to situate Russia at the center of an anti-Western and anti-liberal Eurasian civilization. Such narratives are not just confined to the realm of academia, but permeate political discourses around the world. A view of an Islamic civilization attacked and violated by the West has animated Al Qaeda's rhetoric and given impetus to *Daesh*'s actions. Conservatives in the United States and Europe have likewise portrayed a West under assault by Islam, whether culturally, demographically, or militarily. Donald Trump's 'Muslim ban', for instance, is directly a consequence of these views. Eurasianism is the ideological linchpin of Vladimir Putin's efforts to construct a Eurasian Economic Union juxtaposed with the European Union.

Against narratives and actions of clash, discourses, initiatives and institutions focused on promoting inter-civilizational dialogue and understanding have similarly flourished since the late 1990s. In the UN context, the year 2001 was designated as the Year of the 'Dialogue among Civilizations' on the proposal of then-President of the Islamic Republic of Iran, Mohammed Khatami. This initiative was followed in 2005 by the launch of the UN Alliance of Civilizations, which has since developed a permanent secretariat in New York. In the last 15 years, UNESCO and the Organization for Islamic Cooperation (OIC) have developed actions and programs on dialogue of civilizations. Similarly, many NGOs and interreligious platforms like, for example, the Sant'Egidio Community International Meetings 'Peoples and Religions' and the World Public Forum 'Dialogue of Civilizations', have used the idea of dialogue of civilizations as a vision to counter the dangerous possibilities of clashes. Leaders of very different political, cultural and religious orientations like Václav Havel, Ahmet Davutoglu, and Barack Obama have called for the need for more dialogue and understanding across civilizational lines in international relations.

In short, the notion that we live in a world where civilizations compete or cooperate, potentially clash or hopefully dialogue, has taken hold in international politics today. Why? Why have civilizational imaginaries and narratives become part of everyday international discourses, institutions and practices? Why has this turn towards, what we label as, *civilizational politics* occurred since the end of the Cold War? In other words, why civilizational politics now?

The current literature on civilizations in International Relations (IR) is divided along two dominant perspectives, which we label Primordialist and Critical. Primordialist perspectives, most clearly represented in the writings of Samuel Huntington (1996, 1993), treat civilizations as long-standing, almost-static, essences with clear-cut boundaries and tend towards forms of cultural reductionism. These argue that the crisis of secular ideologies and the process of globalization are intensifying civilizational consciousness and awareness of differences. Critical perspectives, often inspired by the writings of Edward Said (2001; also Said 1978), see civilizations mostly as discourse and tend to privilege a power-based approach. These argue that present-day narratives of civilizational difference are the latest instalment of age-old colonial discourses that seek to divide the West from the Rest and legitimize the former's exercise of power over the latter. Finding both approaches wanting in explaining the rise of civilizational politics in post-Cold War international relations, we build on the most recent scholarship on civilizational analysis (Arnason 2003; Eisenstadt 2003; Katzenstein 2010a) and advance a third Sociological perspective which aims to avoid both cultural and power reductionism while focusing on their crucial relation.

Primordialist and Critical Approaches to Civilizations

Primordialists have presented civilizations as concrete, macro-cultural entities with long, continuous and distinct histories and boundaries, which profoundly structure the way societies, economies, polities and states within them function in the international system. Primordialists' views of civilizations are most clearly articulated in the writings of 'clash of civilizations' theorists, like Huntington, Lewis or Dugin. It is also recognizable to a lesser extent in the writings on the dialogue of civilizations. Especially when it emphasizes the overwhelming centrality of the religious dimension and the view that mutually exclusive and internally monolithic – but not irremediably antagonistic and irreconcilable – religiously-shaped civilizations exist in the world.[1]

By taking Huntington as our main Primordialist voice, how would this perspective explain the rise of civilizational politics in international relations today? For Primordialists the turn towards civilizational imaginaries and narratives in the post-Cold War is explained along two lines. The first is a sort of 'ancient hatreds/Cold War freeze' argument. Civilizations were always there and have always mattered, but we were blinded to this reality by the power of secular ideologies – communism, nationalism, fascism, and liberalism – throughout much of the twentieth century. The century of secular ideologies had temporarily frozen the *forces profondes* of world history. The end of communism and fascism on the one hand, and the crisis of nationalism and liberalism on the other, have opened our eyes to what are our real and truest identities and our most profound traditions and beliefs, those rooted in civilizational belonging and culture (Huntington 1996, 21–28). The second argument is what can be labeled as the 'interaction/friction' argument. The processes of globalization which has taken over the world in the post-Cold War era, has made the world a 'smaller place' (Huntington 1993, 25), causing cultures to rub shoulders ever more closely. Increased interactions, and decreased space for autonomy and maneuver, has ended up intensifying our awareness that, rather than being all alike in a global village, we are actually all different across multiple civilizations and share commonalities within the same one.

There are important problems with this 'back to the future' scenario Primordialists present. Both arguments laid out above point towards some kind of change happening in the post-Cold War, but under-theorize why this change is conducive to bringing to the fore civilizational imaginaries and narratives beyond stating that civilizations have always been there. Have they, though? Where do we see them? We are certainly not aided by the fact

---

[1]   This approach can sometimes be found in the texts and declarations of some interreligious and inter-faith platforms.

that, as Patrick Thaddeus Jackson (2007, 47) pithily puts it, civilizations have 'no front office or central bureaucracy' we can easily turn to or point at. Huntington's definition of civilizations does not help us either since it is one that emphasizes, paradoxically in terms of his own Primordialist perspective, the subjective rather than objective nature of civilizations. Huntington (1993, 24) tells us that civilizations are the 'highest cultural grouping', the largest 'we', that people can use to distinguish one another short of what 'distinguishes humans from other species'. The question then is why do humans need to identify themselves with this particular grouping, after the end of the Cold War? Why aren't, instead, the even larger 'we' of humanity or much narrower local identities drowning out civilizational ones? Why do increased interactions thanks to globalization necessarily accentuate what is different amongst us, rather than what is similar?

While Huntington does gesture to a view of civilizations as constituted by subjective and intersubjective beliefs which evolve over time, he under-theorizes why and how these subjectivities have changed with the end of the Cold War in ways that bring forth the civilizational politics we are witnessing today. In other words, Huntington's cultural reductionism generates what the most recent sociological scholarship on civilizational analysis calls an 'identitarian bias' (Arnason 2003, 4–5), that is an exaggeration of closure and internal unity. As a consequence, a presumed cultural core of civilizations becomes the overwhelming determinant, almost the independent variable, to explain important social, economic and political developments locally and globally. Huntington does not really need to explain the post-Cold War 'return' of civilizational politics, exactly because it is conceived of as a return to a centuries-long 'primordial normality' that had been interrupted by the 'exceptional abnormality' of the short twentieth century of secular ideologies.

The issue here is not to reject a priori an explanatory role for the cultural specificity of civilizations, but to understand the working of cultural patterns in a less deterministic way, avoiding what sometimes are tautological forms of reasoning. For example, take the issue of democracy and its cultural prerequisite: the question should not be about the compatibility or incompatibility of the cultural core of a particular civilization with democracy, a very common framing of the question in recent years in the case of the Islamic civilization. Rather, the question should be framed on the basis of two assumptions. First, the internal differentiation of civilizations some theorists do by talking of civilizational contexts, configurations, constellations, patterns or complexes to indicate a civilization's internal complexity and dynamism (Katzenstein 2010b, 5). Second, the recognition that civilizational contexts can indeed 'set the limits to internal cultural diversity or ideological pluralism' (Arnason 2003, 5). Civilizational contexts generate constraints on the behavior of all actors that operate within this particular cultural frame of reference. But these systemic factors circumscribe a set of possibilities rather than determine specific outputs. In order to explain a particular output – for example the prospects of democracy in a specific Muslim-majority country – a civilizational cultural analysis must be supplemented by an elite-centered analysis of power that makes sense of the struggles (ideological, economic and political) internal to a civilizational context.

Eisenstadt (2003), for example, has shown the centrality of different patterns of dissent, protest and interactions between orthodox and heterodox traditions in understanding civilizational developments. Coming back to our example, the key focus of analysis should be on the relationship between the different competing interpretations of the Islamic legacy and the competition for power of the different groups, constituencies and sectors of societies involved. As a result, the general question of Islam and democracy could be answered by saying that Islam is what Muslims make of it *within* the constraint of its civilizational legacy. At the heart of this analysis we find the role of elites as initiators of change and carriers of innovative cultural projects as well as crucial mediators between cultural patterns and power relations (Eisenstadt 2003; also Arnason 2003).

Where Huntington leaves us in the dark, Critical approaches pick up. These, in fact, see no concrete reality to civilizations except their (inter)subjective ideological nature. Civilizations are ideologies, or better discourses of power, and that is why – Critical perspectives argue – they are so appealing and widely used. Notably articulated in the writing of Edward Said (2001; also Said 1978) and others (Adib-Moghaddam 2011; Hall and Jackson 2007), Critical approaches deconstruct civilizational invocations and narratives as the manifestation of age-old colonial discourses that seek to divide the West from the Rest, produce and reify inclusionary/exclusionary boundaries, and legitimize the West's exercise of power over an 'othered' and 'orientalized' Rest. Even when civilizations are not represented in clash but in dialogue the effect is just as pernicious (Bilgin 2012, see also Sen 2006). That's because, Critical perspectives insist, civilizational invocations help constitute a new form of false consciousness which problematically reifies singular and mutually exclusive belongings that either, on the one hand, overlook the multiple, fluid, and often hybrid identities we all hold or, on the other hand, mask what are instead more fundamental identities and objective disparities around gender, class, race, or power.

Compelling as it is, this Critical approach runs into a number of problems when it comes to explaining today's civilizational politics, however. The first problem, we argue, is that Critical scholars overwhelmingly focus on the role played by civilizational invocations in representing others as enemies. As such, they can hardly explain why dialogue of civilizations narratives – a discourse that 'others' others as friends and partners instead of enemies (Bettiza 2014a, 10–11) – have had a remarkable success, becoming institutionalized in multiple instances.

The second problem is the emphasis Critical perspectives put on civilizational narratives and imaginaries as discourses of power and hegemony. Such a view runs into trouble when we consider that civilizational belonging and ideas are often invoked in world politics with an anti- and counter-hegemonic spirit instead (Bettiza 2014b, 9). This is partly, for instance, the intent of both Mohammad Khatami as well as Osama Bin Laden who, from very different standpoints nonetheless present Islam and the Muslim world as under assault by Western military and cultural power and in need of defense. Immanuel Wallerstein has been one of the few radical scholars to recognize this paradox. In order to explain the new traction of civilizational politics, he has argued that 'the concept of civilizations (plural) arose as a defense against the ravages of civilization (singular)' (Wallerstein 1991, 224). More specifically, in the context of his world-system analysis, civilizational narratives, borrowed from the history of pre-capitalist ancient empires, are meant as identity-boosting devices for the periphery to challenge the cultural liberal hegemony of the core states of the capitalist world system.

Huntington's own thesis is similarly a direct critique of modern liberal notions that Western culture and ideas, and thus by extension also its liberal economic and political projects, are universal and ought to be applied globally. As Huntington (1996, 184; see also Huntington 1993, 39–41) bluntly argues: 'What is universalism to the West is imperialism to the rest'. Indeed, the late Harvard professor does ultimately call for a retrenchment rather than an expansion of Western power and influence internationally (Huntington 1993, 48–49). Our intent here is not to present Huntington as some closeted post-colonial theorist, which he is not. His broad-brush simplifications and cultural determinism are intellectually pernicious, and his portrayal of Islam as having 'bloody borders' (Huntington 1993, 35) oozes prejudice and condescension. The point we are making though, is that civilizational discourses should not be read exclusively as constitutive of hegemonic projects, but also as participating in a politics of contestation and counter-hegemony.

Lastly, Critical perspectives have a further important limit. They cannot explain why such processes of 'othering' – either as enemies or friends – have, since the end of the Cold War, taken the civilizational discursive form and substance they have. The problem here, we find, is that Critical approaches often neglect the wider, extra-discursive social and cultural forces, which have made civilizational imaginaries and narratives resonate so widely across the world since the fall of the Berlin Wall, in comparison to other categories in international politics today. In other words, we are faced with a power reductionism that is the asymmetrical opposite, but has similar logics, to the cultural reductionism of the Primordialist approach. Critical approaches view culture as easily instrumentalized to suit power interests without accounting for the autonomous role of cultural innovation within civilizational traditions as crucial in creating the ideological field of competition among different elite-groups and, therefore, in shaping local and global power structures. Therefore, we contend that an answer to the question of 'why civilizational politics now?' needs to explore and give concrete form to the interplay between cultural patterns and power structures. It is to this exploration – inevitably initial given the limited space – that we now turn.

A Sociological Approach to Civilizations

We suggest a third line of thinking about civilizations, which better helps to explain why we have seen the remarkable and unexpected rise of civilizational politics – the idea that civilizations and their relations matter – in international relations from the 1990s onwards. We label this approach Sociological. Such an approach recognizes that, on the one hand, civilizations are intersubjective phenomena that change and evolve across time; but, on the other, as Peter Katzenstein (2010b, 5) puts it, civilizations should be thought of as 'loosely coupled, internally differentiated, elite-centred social systems that are integrated into a global context'. Hence they cannot be said (*pace* Huntington) to have a historically fixed and culturally distinguishable and invariable essence, which separates them along clear-cut boundaries; yet at the same time their cultural legacies, as we have argued before, constrain and produce structural effects on important socio-political developments beyond their discursive function. Therefore, we treat the meaning and interpretation of civilizations seriously. Unlike Critical approaches, which singularly view civilizations as the instantiation of a particular form of hegemonic discourse, we suggest that because civilizational politics is primarily about the crucial relationship between culture and power synthesized by coalitions of cultural and political elites, wider social, cultural and political forces outside of the discursive realm must be integral to explaining why civilizational imaginaries and narratives are gaining growing salience today.

In particular, we argue that civilizational imaginaries and narratives are becoming more prominent today in world politics for three reasons: (1) they are an expression, in more general terms, of novel forms of identity politics that draw upon culture, religion and tradition; (2) they provide novel 'frames of reference' at a time when globalization contributes to the deterritorialization of national identities, borders and actor-hood; and (3) they constitute political and intellectual critiques of singular conceptions of modernity and liberal universalizing projects, while acting as sites for the articulation of programs of multiple modernities. We will now expand on these three logics that sustain civilizational politics today.

Civilizations as Expressions of Novel Forms of Identity Politics

Civilizational imaginaries and discourses are acquiring salience today because they participate in a form of politics that has come to define our late- or post-modern times; that is, 'identity politics'. This is a politics that does not put the state (like nationalism or fascism), economics (like Marxism, or neo-liberalism), or the individual (like liberalism) first, but identity. Identity politics takes multiple forms. Generally, within more liberal-oriented milieus it focuses on issues of race, gender and sexuality. Within more communitarian-focused approaches, and here where civilizational invocations tend to gain the greatest strength, it focuses on issues of culture, religion and tradition. Drivers of identity politics in the past decades are multiple: globalization and the uncertainties and dislocations this process has brought about; the collapse of universalist ideologies like communism in the wake of the fall of the Berlin wall; and the resurging power and role of religion around the world.

Identity politics expressed through civilizational discourses can take multiple forms. The more pernicious of these are represented by calls for cultural homogeneity, exceptionalism and authoritarianism often put forward by the extreme right, demagogues and populists, or fundamentalist movements. Yet it also can manifest itself in communitarian projects, like those of the dialogue of civilizations, which pose the question of justice in a culturally diverse world and stress the importance of some kind of global multiculturalism based on the recognition, acceptance, and respect of diversity. This is what Charles Taylor (1994) also calls 'the politics of recognition'. The injustice brought about by the lack of recognition of a 'thick' difference and otherness moves attention to the level of identity and introduces a crucial new dimension to politics beyond the understanding of justice as equality (Marxism) or fairness (liberalism). In both cases, civilizational politics is made more prominent by this new philosophical and political centrality that the politics of identity has acquired in a globalized predicament of late/post-modernity where particularism seems to have increasingly stronger normative arguments on its side than universalism.

Civilizations as 'Frames of Reference'

As scholars who see civilizations either as objective facts or as discourses both concur, civilizations cannot be thought of as actors (Huntington 1996; Hall and Jackson 2007). As Fabio Petito (2011, 767), drawing on Johann Arnason, argues, 'civilizations, defined in a fundamentally *culturalist-religious* sense', are reasserting themselves 'as *strategic frames of reference*, not as direct protagonists, of international politics (emphasis in original)'. Civiliz-ations as strategic frames of reference, we suggest, become particularly salient with the end of the Cold War at a moment when globalization contributes to the progressive deterritorialization of national identities, borders and actor-hood. We are living, it is commonly argued, in a world of major and rapid transformations and change (Held 1999), with globalizing processes playing a critical role in dislocating, destabilizing, and pluralizing identities and actors within and beyond the state (Dunn and Goff 2004; Lapid and Kratochwil 1997). Likewise, technological innovations are diffusing power internationally while empowering individuals and non-state actors (Nye 2011, especially Chapter five).

The deterritorialization of identities made possible by globalization produces at the same time apparently contrasting, but arguably mutually reinforcing, outcomes. On the one hand, as Olivier Roy (2010) has highlighted, a hyper-individualization of identity as in the case of new forms of religiosity and conversions where religion is not anymore associated with a specific territorialized culture; on the other, an hyper-collectivization of identity whereby the erosion of territorialized identities is compensated for by the re-politicization of the civilizational identity-marker as macro stabilizer of uncertainty and a sort of order-generating device. Moreover, we are presented today with a bewildering array of agents beyond simply the state that populate the international sphere and participate in important ways in global politics. These range from individuals (bloggers, leakers, entre-preneurs, converts, lone-wolf terrorists, or journalists); to movements and organizations at the civil society level (NGOs, social movements, media outlets, religious institutions, terrorist organizations, or corporations); regional organizations (the European Union (EU), NATO, the Organization for Islamic Cooperation (OIC), or the Association of Southeast Asian Nations (ASEAN)); and international institutions (the UN or the World Bank).

In this context, civilizational imaginaries help map and order along distinct macro-cultural categories an otherwise dizzying range of actors in world politics. Civilizations as strategic frames of reference thus also function as cognitive and intellectual shortcuts which allow observers and participants in world politics to ascribe not just a particular identity, but also certain values and interests to a complex multiplicity of state and non-state actors in international relations. Following this logic then it is possible to view, despite their diversity, Amnesty International, President Trump and NATO as 'Western' and hence promoting Western values and interests; the OIC, Al Qaeda, and President Khatami as constituting multiple voices emanating from the 'Muslim world'; or Gazprom, Dugin and the Russian Orthodox Church as more or less legitimate representatives of the voices and interests not simply of a state, but of a specific culture or civilization. Put differently, ordering the world along civilizations as frames of reference, shifts attention away from a focus solely on inter-state relations. It stresses instead relations among peoples understood as organized politically along different units – be them states, but also sub-state and supra-state actors – who are nonetheless tied together or differentiated from one another by particular macro-cultural identity markers, which are then in turn used to infer specific interests and behaviors.

Civilizations as Normative Critiques

Invocations to civilizations and civilizational politics in international relations, as Critical approaches note, do certainly participate in a range of problematic and exclusionary forms of politics and projects. However, as an intellectual project, theories of civilizational clashes, like those exposed by Huntington, and of dialogues, like those put forward by Mohammad Khatami, Fred Dallmayr, and others (Dallmayr 2002; Hobson 2007; Petito 2007) are generally guided by an important anti-hegemonic ethic. Thus invocations to a world constituted by multiple civilizations, are often part of an intellectual undertaking centered on critiquing liberal teleological, universalist, understandings of progress and modernity, and associated liberal political, economic, and normative projects which originate from the West and are fervently exported, promoted or imposed on the rest of the world.

Moreover, as both Eisenstadt (2003) and Arnason (2003) have suggested, civilizational backgrounds and legacies are the necessary conditions to make sense of the different and varied patterns of modernity. In other words, the plurality of civilizations is the precondition for the pluralization of modernity. From this perspective, modernity is seen as a *sui generis* civilization, not unlike the emergence of the great worldwide religious traditions of Christianity and Islam, consisting, however, of 'a set of infrastructural innovations that can be adapted to diverse civilizational contexts' (Arnason 2003, 34). This is crucial as we will miss a fundamental dimension if we do not recognize that civilizational politics is part of the elite-driven ideological political struggle in contemporary Chinese ('Asian values', Confucian model, etc...), Indian (Hindutva), Russian (Orthodoxy) politics and in the politics of Muslim-majority countries (Islamisms, Sharia law, etc.). Civilizational politics is also about the re-articulation, reinterpretation or even re-invention of civilizational legacies and their core cultural patterns or orientations into contemporary political programs of modernization.

As Fabio Petito (2015) notes, the turn towards civilizational narratives constitutes in part that revolt against the West that Hedley Bull talked about. In particular, such narratives are seen as constituting the fifth and last stage of this revolt: the struggle for cultural liberation – that follows those for sovereign equality, political independence, racial equality, and economic justice. More recently, Petito (2016) has gone further to suggest that civilizational politics should not be confined only to the realm of post-colonial struggles, but also take place in the context of the rise and emergence of a more multipolar world as countries like Russia, China and India re-assert themselves as major powers.

To sum up, the final reason for the post-Cold War growth of civilizational politics, is that it provides an overarching discourse that connects a range of deeply normative critiques of globalization, modernization, Western hegemony and the liberal order with the articulation of different alternative (multiple) ways to deal with the modern predicament. In the international realm, critiques then differ in important ways, however, when articulated along a clash or dialogue perspective.

Clash theorists, like Huntington, see civilizational diversity and cultural pluralism as incommensurable and thus a perennial source of tensions and conflicts. The best that we can hope for, these theorists argue, is prudence and restraint. Scholars and political leaders advancing a civilizational dialogue perspective, instead, generally value cultural pluralism, they see it as a source of enrichment and a key for building a more peaceful and just, less hegemonic or Western/liberal-centric, international order. What is required to reach such a goal, and to dispel narratives of clash, are intercultural and inter-faith dialogues and initiatives across all levels to foster greater understanding, appreciation and cooperation among actors populating an inescapably diverse international community. Similarly, within each civilizational context the reinterpretation of civilizational legacies into alternative paths to development and modernization is rarely uncontested and uniform and more often assumes rather opposed ideological orientations.

Therefore the analysis of the civilizational backgrounds to modernizing processes cannot be only a cultural-historical exercise but it must be also a social analysis of the power dynamics and structures at play.

Conclusion

To conclude, civilizational imaginaries and discourses are a way to understand and practice world politics in the context of a post-Cold War international system marked by: the progressive assertion of culture, tradition and religion as an expression of late/post-modern forms of identity politics; globalization and the deterritorialization of political identities and actorhood; and attempts to resist hegemonic liberal narratives and modernizing projects, while seeking to articulate alternative and multiple modernities.

The new global predicament of identity politics has opened up the space for civilizations to reassert themselves as crucial discursive vectors of contemporary global politics and antagonisms. This requires a highly *power-sensitive* analysis of the new global ideological patterns, as has been rightly pointed out by Critical approaches to civilizations. Civilizations, however, are also operating beyond this discursive dimension as crucial legacies and cultural orientations in the anti-liberal politics of multiple modernities projects. Here a *cultural-based* understanding of civilization is a necessary condition to make sense of the divergent, uneven and different paths of development and modernization around the world. Yet, and crucially *contra* Primordialists, culture alone is not sufficient in identifying social and political outcomes, which are very much influenced by elite-based power struggles and interactions.

Within the limited scope of this paper, the Sociological approach put forward here has thus attempted to outline a way to avoid the limits of both cultural and power reductionisms. It has sought to do so by pointing to the mutually reinforcing relations between civilizations as ideological-strategic frames of reference for global politics and, at the same time, as cultural legacies and orientations for the articulation of programs of alternative modernities. The hope has been to offer some initial analytical tools to better make sense of an international context where civilizational politics are here to stay for the foreseeable future.

References

Adib-Moghaddam, Arshin. 2011. *A Metahistory of the Clash of Civilizations: Us and Them Beyond Orientalism*. London: C. Hurst & Co.

Arnason, Johann P. 2003. *Civilizations in Dispute: Historical Questions and Theoretical Traditions.* Leiden: Brill.

Bettiza, Gregorio. 2014a. "Civilizational Analysis in International Relations: Mapping the Field and Advancing a 'Civilizational Politics' Line of Research." *International Studies Review* 16(1):1–28.

Bettiza, Gregorio. 2014b. "Empty Signifier in Practice: Interrogating the 'Civilizations' of the United Nations Alliance of Civilizations." *European University Institute Working Paper*, RSCAS 2014/95. ReligioWest. http://www. eui.eu/Projects/ReligioWest/Documents/Publications/14SepTBettiza.pdf. Accessed 11 January 2018.

Bilgin, Pinar. 2012. "Civilization, dialogue, security: the challenge of post-secularism and the limits of civilizational dialogue." *Review of International Studies* 38(5):1099–1115.

Dallmayr, Fred R. 2002. *Dialogue Among Civilizations: Some Exemplary Voices*. Basingstoke: Palgrave Macmillan.

Dugin, Aleksandr. 2014. *Eurasian Mission: An Introduction to Neo-Eurasianism*. London: Arktos.

Dunn, Kevin, and Patricia M. Goff. 2004. *Identity and Global Politics: Empirical and Theoretical Elaborations*. New York: Palgrave.

Eisenstadt, Shmuel N. 2003. *Comparative Civilizations and Multiple Modernities. 2 vols.* Leiden and Boston: Brill.

Hall, Martin, and Patrick Thaddeus Jackson, eds. 2007. *Civilizational Identity: the Production and Reproduction of 'Civilizations' in International Relations*. New York, N.Y.: Palgrave Macmillan.

Held, David. 1999. *Global Transformations: Politics, Economics and Culture*. Stanford University Press.

Hobson, John M. 2007. "Deconstructing the Eurocentric Clash of Civilizations: De-Westernizing the West by Acknowledging the Dialogue of Civilizations." In *Civilizational Identity: the Production and Reproduction of 'Civilizations' in International Relations*, edited by Martin Hall and Patrick Thaddeus Jackson, 149–166. New York: Palgrave Macmillan.

Huntington, Samuel P. 1993. "The Clash of Civilizations?." *Foreign Affairs* 72(3): 22–49.

Huntington, Samuel P. 1996. *The Clash of Civilizations and the Remaking of World Order*. New York: Simon & Schuster.

Jackson, Patrick Thaddeus. 2007. "Civilizations as Actors: a Transactional Account." In *Civilizational Identity: the Production and Reproduction of 'Civilizations' in International Relations*, edited by Martin Hall and Patrick Thaddeus Jackson, 33–49. New York: Palgrave Macmillan.

Katzenstein, Peter J., ed. 2010a. *Civilizations in World Politics: Plural and Pluralist Perspectives*. New York: Routledge.

Katzenstein, Peter J. 2010b. "A World of Plural and Pluralist Civilizations: Multiple Actors, Traditions and Practices." In *Civilizations in World Politics: Plural and Pluralist Perspectives*, edited by Peter J. Katzenstein, 1–40. New York: Routledge.

Lapid, Yosef, and Friedrich Kratochwil. 1997. The Return of Culture and Identity in IR Theory. Boulder, Co: Lynne Rienner Publishers.

Lewis, Bernard. 2002. *What Went Wrong? The Clash Between Islam and Modernity in the Middle East*. London: Weidenfeld & Nicholson.

Nye, Joseph S. 2011. *The Future of Power*. PublicAffairs.

Petito, Fabio. 2007. "The Global Political Discourse of Dialogue among Civilizations: Mohammad Khatami and Václav Havel." *Global Change, Peace & Security* 19(2): 103–126.

Petito, Fabio. 2011. "In Defence of Dialogue of Civilizations: with a Brief Illustration of the Diverging Agreement Between Edward Said and Louis Massignon." *Millennium: Journal of International Studies* 39(3): 759–779.

Petito, Fabio. 2015. "The contemporary ambiguities of religions as a source of civilizational identity." In *Nations Under God: The Geopolitics of Faith in the Twenty-First Century*, edited by Luke Herrington, Alasdair McKay and Jeffrey Haynes, 63–70. Bristol, UK: E-International Relations.

Petito, Fabio. 2016. "Dialogue of Civilizations in a Multipolar World: Towards a Multicivilizational-Multiplex World Order." *International Studies Review* 18(1): 78–91.

Roy, Olivier. 2010. *Holy Ignorance: When Religion and Culture Part Ways*. New York: Columbia/Hurst.

Said, Edward. 2001. "The Clash of Ignorance." *The Nation*.

Said, Edward W. 1978. *Orientalism*. London: Penguin [2003].

Sen, Amartya. 2006. *Identity and Violence: the Illusion of Destiny*. New York: W. W. Norton & Co.

Taylor, Charles. 1994. "The Politics of Recognition." In *Multiculturalism: Examining the Politics of Recognition*, edited by Amy Gutmann, 25–73. Princeton: Princeton University Press.

Wallerstein, Immanuel. 1991. *Geopolitics and Geoculture: Essays on the Changing World-System*. Cambridge: Cambridge University Press.

Zakaria, Fareed and Lee Kuan Yew. 1994. "Culture Is Destiny: A Conversation with Lee Kuan Yew." *Foreign Affairs* 73(2): 109–126.

5

Huntington's 'Clash of Civilizations' Today: Responses and Developments

JEFFREY HAYNES

It is now a quarter of a century since Samuel Huntington first published his treatise about what he understood as an epochal event in international relations: the post-Cold War 'clash of civilizations'.

Since the late 1970s, the talk has been of the impossibility of different sets of values, norms and beliefs living side-by-side in an increasingly globalized world. In 1993, the late Samuel Huntington published one of the most cited articles in international relations literature: 'The Clash of Civilizations?' (*Foreign Affairs*, Summer 1993, pp. 22–48), followed three years later by a book-length treatment of the same issue. Why are the article and book so important for our understanding of the post-Cold War world? Why are they collectively a touchstone for nearly all contemporary debates about the capacity of different groups to live together in relative amity not enmity?

Origins and Development of the Clash of 'Clash of Civilizations'

Bernard Lewis (1990), the British orientalist, was the first to claim there was a 'clash between civilizations' in a speech at Johns Hopkins University in 1957. Lewis argued that Islam and the West had differing values which would only be resolved following conflict. Initially, however, Lewis's contention did not create much of a stir. This was hardly surprising given that the main foreign policy issue confronting the West in the late 1950s was dealing with what was widely perceived as an expansionist Soviet Union. Four decades later, Lewis's clash *between* civilizations had become a clash *of* civilizations. This was the claim of Samuel Huntington, who contended that a clash between the West and the 'Muslim world' would be the key foreign policy issue for the US (and the West more generally) after the 1991 breakup of the Soviet Union. Like Lewis, 40 years earlier, Huntington argued that one of the two 'sides' was ideationally destined to prevail over the over. Because of their differing values, it would not be possible for them to unite to defeat humanity's myriad common problems (such as climate change, poverty, and gender inequality).

The relationship between a scholarly argument relating to, and popular understanding of, a phenomenon is not always clear. Had things turned out differently, Huntington's arguments on the 'clash of civilizations' would probably have been debated only by a few scholars, without much impact on policy-makers or popular understanding of how the world works. But the events of 9/11 made Huntington's arguments mainstream and centre stage. The 9/11 attacks had been preceded by others which, with hindsight, could be seen as initial signs of a 'civilizational war' between the West and the Muslim world. A first jihadi assault on the Twin Towers in 1993 was followed in 1998 by attacks on two US embassies in Africa. The 1993 and 1998 attacks, coupled with 9/11, seemed to some to be clear signs that Islamist extremists were willing to take the 'clash of civilizations' to the stage of open conflict with the US. Neither President George W. Bush nor President Barack Obama responded to terrorism carried out by actors motivated by Islamist ideologies by declaring war on 'Islam'. President Bush stated a week after 9/11 that '[t]hese acts of violence against innocents violate the fundamental tenets of the Islamic faith'. The US response, Bush decreed, was to go to war with al-Qaeda terrorists, whose words and deeds perverted 'the peaceful teaching of Islam' (Bush 2001). A few years later, Obama also denied that there was a 'clash of civilizations' between the US and the Muslim world. In a major speech in Cairo in 2009, not long after assuming the presidency, Obama sought to reach out to Muslim-majority societies, aiming to set relations on an improved footing (Obama 2009). However, neither Bush nor Obama was successful in preventing a 'clash of civilizations' mentality from spreading and gaining strength at the popular level in America, especially among those who identify with the political and religious right. Right-wing political media such as Fox News and certain politically conservative evangelical leaders became more and more bluntly critical of Islam with each passing year.

By the time of the presidential campaign in 2016, the issue of the relationship between the US and the Muslim-majority world was very much in the spotlight. During the electoral process, the republican candidate for president, Donald Trump, stated (among many other things) that 'I think Islam hates us' (2017). There was no attempt to clarify that he was referring only to 'radical Islamic terrorists' (Trump 2017). Few on the hard-right thought he needed to offer any clarification or qualification.

My argument in this brief piece is not that Huntington's article and book were so important because his argument was 'correct' or 'right'. My claim is twofold: First, Huntington's article was and is important because it captured perfectly the end-of-the-Cold War *zeitgeist*, a way of seeing the world which has endured in the uncertain years which have followed, as exemplified by the hostility shown to 'Islam' by candidate (now President) Trump. Second, Huntington's argument has proved to be an abiding statement about globalisation and the hopes and fears that it conveys. It is almost irrelevant that his focal point: the impossibility of the West – read; the US – and 'Islam' – read; 'Islamic radicalism/fundamentalism' – living together in harmony was laughingly over-simplified, redolent of the paranoia of someone experiencing the shattering of a stable, safe and unchanging world suddenly and demonstrably confronted with the scenario of the post-World War II paradigm smashed to smithereens. What was a card-carrying Realist, such as Huntington, to do under these circumstances? The response was to find a new enemy and dress it up in the same preposterous 'baddy' clothes that had marked the treatment by US Realists of the Soviet Union from the start of the Cold War in the late 1940s and transfer the characteristics of conflict to a new 'actor': 'Islamic fundamentalism.'

It may be worth recalling that a quarter century ago in the early 1990s, the world was just emerging from a 50-year period of secular ideological polarization, focused on the US and the Soviet Union, the poster children of very different worldviews: 'liberal democracy' and 'global communism'. Contrary to today's triumphalist claims of some in the US, the US did not 'win' the Cold War; rather, the Soviet Union 'lost' it. Unable to compete with America in a competition for global dominance, its shaky, dysfunctional and misanthropic political/social/economic system spectacularly imploded within a seemingly impossibly short period of time: apparently as strong as ever in the mid-1980s, by 1991, the Soviet Union and its system as well as its parasitic coterie of attendant nations were no more. This left a gulf, a hole, a vacuum. How, and with what, to fill it?

Globalization, redolent of democracy, capitalism and freedom, was the heady force which defeated the USSR. In addition, globalization was also the factor which reinjected religion back into international relations, having been forced in the centuries following the Peace of Westphalia in 1648 into marginal-ization. The sudden demise of the Cold War, as well as the Soviet Union and its attendant secular ideology, opened the way for a new focus on 'culture' and 'civilizations', of which religion is very often an integral aspect. The 9/11 attacks on the United States were a key event in the debate about the role of cultural and religious difference – especially, 'Islamic fundamentalism' – in international conflict, especially in the way that they focused attention on al-Qaeda's then dominant brand of globalized cultural terrorism. For some scholars, analysts and policy makers – especially but not exclusively in the United States – 9/11 marked the practical onset of Samuel Huntington's 'clash of civilizations' between two cultural entities: the 'Christian West' and the 'Islamic world', with special concern directed at Islamic 'fundamentalists' or 'radical terrorists'. This is not to suggest that Huntington's arguments have had it all their own way. For some, 9/11 was not the *start* of a 'clash of civilizations' but rather the *last gasp* of transnational Islamist radicalism. (It remains to be seen if still unfolding events in Mali, Niger, Nigeria and elsewhere are the start of a new phase of Islamist radicalism.) On the other hand, it is hard to disagree with the claim that the events of September 11 thrust culture to the forefront of the international agenda, providing Huntington's thesis with a new lease of life. Henceforward, many commentators were no longer inhibited in attributing essentialist character-istics to the 'Christian West' and 'Islam'. After 9/11, there was a pronounced penchant to see the world in a Huntington-inspired simplistic division, with straight lines on maps – 'Islam has bloody borders', Huntington averred (1993, 35) – apparently the key to understanding what were increasingly portrayed as definitively ethically and racially defined lines across the globe.

September 11, 2001, as well as many subsequent terrorist outrages, were perpetrated by al-Qaeda or its followers; all involved extremist Muslims that wanted to cause destruction and loss of life against 'Western' targets that nevertheless often led to considerable loss of life, for example in Istanbul and Casablanca, among Muslims. The US response – the Bush administration's 'war on terror' – targeted Muslims, some believe rather indiscriminately, in Afghanistan, Iraq and elsewhere. Some have claimed that these events 'prove' the correctness of Huntington's thesis. In such views, the 9/11 attacks and the US response suggested that Huntington's prophecy about clashing civilizations was now less abstract and more plausible than when first articulated in the early 1990s.

Others contend, however, that 9/11 was not the start of the 'clash of civilizations' – but, as already noted, the last gasp of radical Islamists' attempts to foment revolutionary change which had begun with Iran's revolution in 1979 and carried on into the 1980s with determined attempts by Islamist radicals to gain state power in Algeria and Egypt. We can also note, however, that 9/11 not only had major effects on both the US and international relations but also contributed to a surge of Islamic radicalism in Saudi Arabia. This was a result not only of the presence of US troops in the kingdom, as highlighted by al-Qaeda's then leader, the late Osama bin Laden, but also due to a growing realization that the function of Saudi Arabia's *ulema* was and is overwhelmingly to underpin and explain away the unearned and unrepresentative dominance of the ruling king, his extended family and parasitic entourage.

The United Nations' and 'Moderate' Muslims' Response to the 'Clash of Civilizations'

Huntington's argument about the 'clash of civilizations' coincided with what some have called the 'return' of religion to international relations. Higher profile for religion in international relations was manifested in various ways, including an increasing presence at the world's only global intergovernmental organization, the United Nations (UN). The role of religion at the UN expanded greatly after 9/11. The UN itself instituted a new entity in 2005: the Alliance of Civilizations (UNAOC), whose name was a direct riposte to Huntington's argument about the inevitability of civilizations clashing in the post-Cold War world. The UNAOC was created by the UN General Assembly and headed by the UN Secretary-General, following a request from the governments of Spain and Turkey. This is not to imply that the UN suddenly 'got' religion after decades of secular focus or that the UN is now the focus of a single, coordinated faith voice. Indeed, UNAOC's concern with civilizational disharmony is itself a manifestation of difference in this regard. A major analytical controversy in this regard is what is meant by the term 'civilization' and how do such entities act in international relations, including at the UN. For example, while today inter-civilizational tensions and conflicts are typically linked to the perceived polarizing effects of globalization, half a century ago the focus was on different values between the West and secular Arab nationalists. When Bernard Lewis coined the phrase 'clash between civilizations' six decades ago, he was referring to a then extant ideological issue, that is, the baleful relationship of contemporary Arab nationalists, such as Egypt's Gamal Abdel Nasser, who led the country between 1956 until his death in 1970, and who frequently expressed hostility towards the West. By the early 1990s, the focus had changed from secular nationalist hostility to Western security concerns with 'Islamic fundamentalism'.

Petito (2007; 2009) notes that, partly in response to Huntington's claims of civilizational conflict, a counter narrative emerged stressing how vitally important it is for harmonious international relations that there is improved dialogue to deter a 'clash of civilizations'. A key milestone in this regard came in 1998, when the then-president of Iran, Seyed Muhammad Khatami, called for improved 'dialogue among civilizations' during an address to the UN General Assembly. Following Khatami's call, the General Assembly designated 2001 as the Year of Dialogue among Civilizations, an initiative strongly supported by the UN's Educational, Scientific and Cultural Organization (UNESCO). Yet, before Khatami's initiative could firmly take root and develop, his efforts were derailed by the 9/11 attacks on the World Trade Center and Pentagon. They were quickly followed by the US-led invasions of Afghanistan (2001) and Iraq (2003) which de facto killed Khatami's 'dialogue among civilizations' idea. Yet, international concern was too pronounced to give up on the idea of improved dialogue between civilizations and before long the Alliance of Civilizations initiative was announced under the auspices of the UN.[1] The UNAOC was initially suggested in 2004 at the 59th Session of the UN General Assembly by the then Prime Minister of Spain, José Luis Rodriguez Zapatero, supported by Recep Tayyip Erdoğan, Turkey's prime minister at the time. The UNAOC was formally launched a year later by the UN Secretary General at the time, Kofi Annan. In 2007, Annan's successor, Ban Ki-moon, appointed a former president of Portugal, Jorge Sampaio, as head of UNAOC. Sampaio held the position until September 2012, when he was replaced by Qatar's Nassir Abdulaziz Al-Nasser, a former leader of the UN General Assembly, who took up the role in March 2013.

UNAOC prioritizes building 'a global network of partners including States, International and regional organizations, civil society groups, foundations, and the private sector to improve cross-cultural relations between diverse nations and communities' (2017c). To this end, a 'Group of Friends' supports UNAOC, comprising, at the time of writing (October 2017), 120 governments and 26 international organizations (IOs) (2017a). In addition, UNAOC has 'memorandums of understanding' with 16 'Partner Organizations', including some IOs also listed in the Group of Friends[2], such as the Council of Europe and the Organization of Islamic Cooperation (OIC), and some entities which are not, including the Anna Lindh Foundation, the Global Dialogue Foundation and La Francophonie (2017b). The aim of UNAOC reaching out to both state and non-state actors is to highlight its focus: not appearing to be solely a UN-focused, top-down body, remote from the concerns of governments, NGOs and 'ordinary' people. The overall aim is to roll back a putative or real 'clash of civilizations' and instead develop enhanced dialogue between cultural and religious groups for mutual, long-term benefit.

While the UN has sought fit to establish an entity with the express purpose of repudiating Huntington's 'clash of civilizations', 'moderate' Muslims have also responded to his contention by stressing the common 'moderate' ground which Christians and Muslims occupy. Kamali (2015, 9) argues that there are strong injunctions to moderation within the Islamic tradition:

---

[1]   It did not help that Khatami was a former president of Iran during an era when relations between Iran and the West, especially the US, became strained as a result of Iran's nuclear power aspirations.

[2]   'A *Group of Friends* is a usual practice both in the UN framework and in other international arenas by which the country which is sponsoring a particular international initiative – whereas it is Spain and Turkey at the Alliance of Civilizations process, Finland with the Helsinki Process, or Canada in the Responsibility to Protect – creates an informal group with those other member states supportive of the initiative to promote it, give support and content and ensure its advance in the agenda of the different intergovernmental bodies' (Manonelles, 2007: fn. 3).

Wasatiyyah ('moderation') is an important but somewhat neglected aspect of Islamic teachings that has wide-ranging ramifications in almost all areas of concern to Islam. 'Moderation' is primarily a moral virtue of relevance not only to personal conduct of individuals but also to the integrity and self-image of communities and nations. Moderation is an aspect, in its Qur'anic projections, of the self-identity and worldview of the Muslim community, or *ummah*.

There have been several attempts since the early 2000s to pursue initiatives both within the Muslim world and in interfaith contexts, with the aim of highlighting and pursuing the path of 'moderation', to improve interfaith relations between Muslims and Christians. Several initiatives highlighting *wasatiyyah* followed 9/11: six institutional developments and four non-institutionalized initiatives. The institutional developments were: (1) International Assembly for Moderate Islamic Thought and Culture (based in Jordan, 2003); (2) International Centre for Moderation (Kuwait, 2004); (3) Centre for Islamic Moderation and Renewal (Doha, 2008); (4) Global Movement of Moderates Foundation (Malaysia, 2012); (5) Institute Wasatiyyah Malaysia (Malaysia, 2013); and (6) International Institute of Wasatiyyah (Malaysia, 2013). The four non-institutionalized initiatives were: (1) The Islamic Scholars and Religious Teachers Association Charter of Moderation in Religious Practice (Singapore, 2003); (2) The Mecca Declaration (Saudi Arabia, 2005); (3) The Amman Message (Jordan, 2005); and (4) 'A Common Word between Us and You' (Jordan, 2007). These and other interfaith and inter-civilizational initiatives and reform measures are significant not only because of their ideas and orientations stressing moderation – in contrast to the 'clash of civilizations' thesis which stresses the lack of moderation and common ground between civilizations – but also because they explicitly expose incorrect, entrenched perceptions, such as: Islam is incapable of change; Islam is a violent religion; Muslims do not speak out against religious extremism and terrorism; and all Muslims reject religious pluralism and interfaith dialogue (Kamali 2015, 80).

The overall impact of assertions of Islamic 'moderation' is difficult or impossible to gauge accurately. However, one of the initiatives, 'A Common Word between Us and You', an open letter dated 13 October 2007, turned out to be controversial. The letter was organized and sent out by Jordan's Royal Aal al-Bayt Institute for Islamic Thought. It was signed by 138 influential Muslim leaders and scholars from around the world, 'from a wide variety of denominations and schools of thought within Islam, and addressed to the contemporary leadership of Christian Churches, federations and organizations' (Marciewicz 2016, 23). It was clearly an attempt to stress the importance of common ground between the faiths and to try to undermine the 'clash of civilizations' argument.

The open letter called for peace between Muslim and Christians, contending that followers of both faiths should try to work together to find common ground between them. This is in line with the Qur'anic decree: 'Say: O People of the Scripture? Come to a common word between us and you: that we worship none but God' (Qur'an, Chapter three, Verse 64). It also accords with the Biblical commandment to love God and one's neighbour (Matthew, Chapter 22, Verses 37 and 39). The open letter set in train a spirited interfaith dialogue between Christians and Muslims. In 2008 'A Common Word' was awarded the Eugen Biser Award, given by a German foundation, and the Building Bridges Award from the UK-based Association of Muslim Social Scientists ('"A Common Word" Receives AMSS (UK)' 2008). The initiative did not attract support from all Christians. According to Pavlischek (2008, 61), this was because, following 'the initial flurry of responses following its publication in November 2007, more careful measure has been taken of "Loving God and Neighbor"'. Pavlischek, an evangelical Christian, writing in the pages of *The Review of Faith & International Affairs*, contends that 'A Common Word' received 'withering theological criticism', including its ignoring of the crucial issue of religious liberty. Pavlischek notes that while the Royal Aal Al-Bayt Institute was sending out 'A Common Word' it was simultaneously issuing 'fatwas denouncing apostates on a website it sponsors'.

The open letter was published in October 2007. By February 2008, the fatwas to which Pavlischek refers had been removed from the website (Durie 2008). The Royal Aal Al-Bayt Institute for Islamic Thought (2009) issued a summary document on the open letter, which also included a commentary. It stated that '*takfir* (declarations of apostasy) between Muslims' are forbidden. It is not known why the fatwas were removed. However, for some Christians, this was the most crucial aspect of the open letter, highlighting what appeared to be a fundamental difference between Christians and Muslims and which supported the 'clash of civilizations' argument that the values of the different worldviews (Western and Muslim) were so different as to make the finding of common ground difficult or even impossible. Pavlischek (2008) argued that whereas Christians assert 'the right of individual human beings to choose, proclaim, and change their religion without fear of legal sanctions', in Islam there is nothing like the same freedom to move to another religion. In short, the issue of religious freedom is one of the main critiques of Islam from Christians. This is because, as Marshall (2016) explains, 'major factors in contemporary Christian persecution [include] Christianity's virtually intrinsic association with pluralism and freedom' (Paul Marshall 2016, quoted in Philpott and Shah 2017, 4).

Conclusion

What of the goal of improved cross-cultural relations between diverse nations and communities, in direct riposte to Huntington's 'clash of civilizations' argument? Historically, neither the Christian/Western nor Muslim worlds have worked assiduously to achieve improved inter-civilizational dialogue and bridge building. Yet, a new and mutually rewarding relationship has the potential to emerge between the Muslim and Christian worlds, where accumulated wisdom and insights for necessary progress provide the basis of a valued coexistence. After 9/11, it is clear that such an improved relationship would be premised not on ideas of cultural superiority, but on mutual respect and openness to cultural eclecticism. In other words, Muslims and Christians can learn from each other and cooperate in the pursuit of shared values. The goal is to engage meaningfully and consistently in inter-civilizational bridge-building so as to develop and deepen normatively desirable values and expand common understandings of truth, to transform an increasingly conflict-filled relationship to one with collective good works serving humanity and the demonstration of the soundness of common values and contribution to civilizations (Said 2002, 7). It remains a moot point, however, the extent to which the pursuit – and the finding – of common ground between the West and the Muslim world is destined to replace the confrontational rhetoric of Huntington's 'clash of civilizations'. We have seen that both the UN and 'moderate' Muslims have stressed that interreligious and intercultural dialogue is the way forward. But, will politicians like Donald Trump listen and act accordingly?

References

Bush, George W. 2001. "'Islam Is Peace', Says President." Remarks by the President at Islamic Center of Washington, D.C. *The White House*, 17 September. https://georgewbush-whitehouse.archives.gov/news/releases/2001/09/20010917-11.html Accessed 12 April 2017.

Durie, Mark. 2008. "The Apostasy Fatwas and 'A Common Word Between Us and You'." http://acommonword.blogspot.de/2008/02/apostasy-fatwas-and-common-word-between.html Accessed 12 April 2017.

Huntington, Samuel. 1993. "The Clash of Civilizations?" *Foreign Affairs* 72 (Summer): 22–49.

Huntington, Samuel. 1996. *The Clash of Civilizations and the Remaking of World Order*. New York: Simon & Schuster.

"I Think Islam Hates Us." 2017. The Editorial Board, *The New York Times* 26 January: A28.

Kamali, Mohammad Kashim. 2015. *The Middle Path of Moderation in Islam.* New York: Oxford University Press.

Lewis, Bernard. 1990. "The Roots of Muslim Rage." *The Atlantic*, September, 266(3): 47–60.

Manonelles, Manuel. 2007. "Peace Human Rights." *Pace Diritti Umani*, No. 1, January–April. http://unipd-centrodirittiumani.it/public/docs/PDU1_2007_A041.pdf Accessed 27 October 2017.

Markiewicz, Sara. 2016. *World Peace Through Christian-Muslim Understanding.* Göttingen: V&R unipress GmbH.

Marshall, Paul. 2016. "Patterns and Purposes of Contemporary Anti-Christian Persecution." In *Christianity and Freedom: Volume 2, Contemporary Perspectives*, edited by Allen Hertzke and Timothy Samuel Shah, 58–86. New York: Cambridge University Press.

Obama, Barack. 2009. "The President's Speech in Cairo: A New Beginning." *The White House*, 4 June. https://obamawhitehouse.archives.gov/blog/2009/06/04/presidentrsquos-speech-cairo-a-new-beginning Accessed 12 April 2017.

Pavlischek, Keith. 2008. "Why I Would Not Have Signed the Yale Response to 'A Common Word'." *The Review of Faith & International Affairs* 6(4): 61–63.

Petito, Fabio. 2007. "The Global Political Discourse of Dialogue among Civilizations: Mohammad Khatami and Vaclav Havel." *Global Change, Peace & Security,* 19(2): 103–25.

Philpott, Daniel and Timothy Samuel Shah. 2017. "In Response to Persecution: Essays from the Under Caesar's Sword Project." *The Review of Faith and International Affairs* 15(1): 1–11.

The Royal Aal Al-Bayt Institute. 2009. *The Amman Message.* Amman: Royal Islamic Strategic Studies Centre.

Said, Abdul. 2002. "The Whole World Needs the Whole World: Establishing a Framework for a Dialogue of Civilizations." Washington, DC: The American University.

Trump, Donald. 2017. "The Inaugural Address." *The White House,* 20 January. https://www.whitehouse.gov/inaugural-address Accessed 12 April 2017.

The United Nations Alliance of Civilizations. 2017a. "Group of Friends Members." http://www.unaoc.org/who-we-are/group-of-friends/members/ Accessed 14 November 2017.

The United Nations Alliance of Civilizations. 2017b. "Partner Organizations." http://www.unaoc.org/who-we-are/partner-organizations/ Accessed 14 November 2017.

The United Nations Alliance of Civilizations. 2017c. "Who We Are." http://www.unaoc.org/who-we-are/ Accessed 14 November 2017.

6

The Kin-Country Thesis Revisited

KIM RICHARD NOSSAL

One of the key features of Samuel Huntington's world of clashing civilizations was the phenomenon of 'kin-country rallying'. States that were part of the civilization, Huntington argued, were like kin, and, more importantly, behaved like kin. Kin-countries, he argued, were a crucial part of the 'remaking' of global politics in the post-Cold War era. Indeed, the introduction of 'kin' relationships in international relations was a novel feature in a broader idea that was already widely seen as 'novel and jarring' (Betts 2010, 188).

The purpose of this chapter is to revisit the idea of kin-country in contemporary international relations. I argue that the novelty of kin-country rallying in the 1990s when Huntington first outlined his 'new' approach to world politics (Huntington 1993, 35–39) was largely because his identification of the dynamics of kinship in world politics challenged the core assumptions of international relations theory that was so dominant in the American academy at the time. By contrast, for those outside the United States, the phenomenon of kin-country was historically familiar, even if, like Molière's Monsieur Jourdain, who was delighted to discover that he had been speaking prose all his life without knowing it, they had not been using the language of kin-country. I conclude, however, that while Huntington's kin-country approach provides a much clearer way to understand the relations among some countries than orthodox international relations theory, it is unlikely to be used, since it is so intimately identified with the broader civilizational clash thesis.

The Kin-Country Syndrome

When Huntington was writing his *Foreign Affairs* article in late 1992, an article in the *Boston Globe* caught his eye. H.D.S. Greenway, at the time the senior associate editor of the newspaper, noted that the war that was raging in Bosnia was having ripple effects far beyond the Balkans. Greenway was reporting on an emergency meeting of the Organization of the Islamic Conference (as the Organization of Islamic Cooperation was known before 2011), being held in Jeddah. The OIC was seeking to redress the military balance between the Bosnian Serbs and the Bosnian Muslims by having a United Nations arms embargo lifted. Greenway noted that this was a good example of the 'complicating factor' of the relationship between 'an ethnic group and its kin country' (Greenway 1992).

Greenway provided a number of other examples. He argued that the Russians had on numerous occasions intervened in the Balkans to protect Orthodox Christian Slavs, going so far as to suggest that 'if the Russians had not mobilized to stop Austrian bullying of Serbia in 1914, World War I might have been prevented'. He noted that both Greece and Turkey were deeply engaged with what he called 'their kinsmen' in Cyprus. Britain found itself similarly engaged in Northern Ireland. Russians continued to be engaged in the politics of the former Soviet republics over mistreatment of Russians in those countries. Serbia was a 'hostage to the Serbs in Bosnia', with the government of Slobodan Milošević manipulating the Bosnian Serb minority 'as Berlin manipulated the Sudetan Germans in the 1930s'. Greenway had a catchy phrase for what was going on in Jeddah, a phrase that appeared in the headline of the article: the 'kin-country syndrome'.

Huntington took Greenway's phrase and expanded on the idea of family, and built kinship relations into his civilizational argument. However, it should be noted that unlike many of the other elements of his civilizational argument, which were often well-grounded in theoretical and empirical works in the field, Huntington did not explicitly ground his discussion of kinship in either the original *Foreign Affairs* article, or the 1996 book that flowed from it, in any of the huge extant literature on kinship (for a review of late-twentieth century theoretical literature on kinship, see Peletz 1995). Instead, he just used the terms kin, kinship and kin-country without further elaboration; no doubt he assumed that his readers would use their own understandings of what kin, kinship and kin-country might involve. As a result, without a theoretically-grounded understanding of kinship, it is never precisely clear what drives the ties that create the kin-country syndrome. Using Greenway's example of the Jeddah meeting of the CIO in December 1992 that so inspired Huntington, it is not clear whether the 'kinship' observed there was driven by descent, religion, culture, identity, nationality, national interest, or a shared member-ship in a common civilization. Huntington, needless to say, would have argued the latter, but, as critics note, that is precisely one of the enduring flaws of the civilizational argument: actually defining those civilizations.

Huntington, however, seemed untroubled by this lack of definitional and theoretical rigor. Clearly working on the assumption that readers would know kinship when they saw it, he sketched out the essence of the kin-country syndrome and how it would affect global politics in the future. Central to the discussion was, of course, the identification of civilization as the core focus of global conflict after the end of the Cold War between competing ideologies. And while Huntington (1996, 44) averred that civilizations were cultural rather than political entities, he nonetheless argued that what he called 'core states' within civilizations played a central political role:

> In the emerging global politics, the core states of the major civilizations are supplanting the two Cold War superpowers as the principal poles of attraction and repulsion for other countries.... States in these civilizational blocs often tend to be distributed in concentric circles around the core state or state, reflecting their degree of identification with and integration into that bloc (Huntington 1996, 154).

In a world of civilizations, Huntington suggested, 'the core states of civilizations are the sources of order within civilizations and, through negotiations with other core states, between civilizations' (1996, 156). Within civilizations, order is created because of ties of kinship:

> A core state can perform its ordering function because member states perceive it as a cultural kin. A civilization is an extended family and, like older members of a family, core states provide their relatives with both support and discipline (1996, 156).

Huntington argued that the kinship felt by people in different nations within a civilization has significant political effects. In particular, 'in civilizational conflicts, unlike ideological ones, kin stand by their kin' (1996, 217). This leads to 'kin-country rallying' (1996, 20) – or as he called it in the *Foreign Affairs* article 'civilization rallying' (1993, 35) – which is marked by 'efforts by a state from one civilization to protect kinsmen in another civilization' (1996, 208). This rallying involves both governments and peoples: in some cases, diasporas will take the lead in organizing support – financial, military, and political – for their civilizational 'kin'; in other cases, governments will be the prime movers.

Such kin-country rallying, Huntington contends, will have a critical impact on contemporary global conflict. In a world of nation-states, Huntington contended, conflicts between states will be largely limited to the protagonists, or those with a deep and direct interest in devoting blood and treasure to the cause. Nations X and Y might go to war with each other, but the likelihood of widening that conflict is highly limited. In a world of civilizations, by contrast, the dynamics of kin-country rallying have the effect of widening wars. When wars break out on what Huntington called the 'fault lines' of civilizations (1993, 29–35; 1996, 207–208), local groups A1 and B1 will fight each other, but each will seek 'to expand the war and mobilize support from civilizational kin groups, A2, A3, A4, and B2, B3, and B4, and those groups will identify with their fighting kin' (1996, 254). Moreover, contemporary transportation and communications make the internationalization of kin-country support easier to accomplish: money, goods, services, arms, and even people are moved effortlessly across national boundaries.

Huntington sought to provide evidence for his kin-country rallying thesis in both the *Foreign Affairs* article and his book. Following the lead originally provided by Greenway in 1992, he examined the war in Yugoslavia, and the willingness of groups and states to rally around the different warring parties during the course of the 1990s. He was able to point to numerous diasporas, particularly those in Western countries, that rallied to support their 'kinfolk' back home. In the 1990s, ethnic conflicts in the former Yugoslavia, the former Soviet Union, Indonesia and the countries of the Middle East appeared to confirm the thesis, at least superficially.

But on closer examination, it is clear that there was in fact not as much civilization rallying as Huntington asserted. In a critique written two years before the book appeared, Richard E. Rubenstein and Jarle Crocker noted just how selective Huntington was in the cases of rallying he presented, ignoring the ethnic and national conflicts that had raged in the Soviet Union for two decades before the end of the Cold War, or choosing to focus only on those ethno-national conflicts in the Middle East or Africa that proved his thesis while ignoring others. As Rubenstein and Crocker put it crisply, 'that selectivity will not wash' (1994, 121).

Moreover, because of the wonky way that Huntington defined the eight major civilizations that are supposed to comprise contemporary global politics, it is not at all clear that transnational conflicts, even at the so-called 'fault lines' between civilizations – fault lines that run suspiciously along the borders of sovereign nation-states – were inter-civilizational conflicts. However, while Huntington's claims of kin-country rallying were clearly overstated, it can be argued that his identification of kinship as a factor in global politics – even if under-theorized – was a novel departure from the dominant orthodoxies of international relations theory in the 1990s.

Kin-Countries in World Politics

Huntington's identification of sentiments of 'kinship' across national borders – and in particular the existence of 'kin-countries' – stood in stark contrast to the orthodox theorizing in international politics about the relations of independent political communities dominant at the time that Huntington was writing – realism. While there were – and are – different strands of realism, all variants share a common assumption that independent political communities are atomistic, self-regarding, and fundamentally selfish in their relations with all other political communities.

The most durable realist is Hans J. Morgenthau (1948; 2005), whose path-breaking work in the late 1940s was so dominant during the Cold War era that it was still being revised and used as an IR text in 2005, fully 25 years after his death in 1980. Morgenthau's classic conception of international relations was that world politics was little more than the endless struggles of self-interested units seeking to avoid domination by others in an environment that is fundamentally anarchic and comparable to a Hobbesian state of nature, where there was no government, and thus where everyone treated one another as an enemy. In this view, the units may take different forms over time – since 1648, they have predominantly been sovereign nation-states – but the essence of their interaction is unchanging over time: they define their interests in terms of power and struggle with each other to seek a balance of power.

There were critiques of Morgenthau's classical realist perspective. For example, Keohane and Nye (1977) argued that the classical realist portrait did neither describe nor explain the relations between the United States and its European allies in the 1970s. That relationship, they argued, was not determined by raw power politics; rather, they argued that there was a 'complex' degree of interdependence between the US and Western Europe, and this changed the nature of their relationship: their economic and security relationship altered the way that power was exercised across the Atlantic. Likewise, English School theorists like Hedley Bull (1977) argued that classical realist theory did not capture the degree to which politics between independent political communities invariably sought to establish a social order, and that while sovereign nation-states in the contemporary system may be self-seeking, global politics was far removed from the kind of grim Hobbesian state of nature painted by classical realists.

Another important strand was the elaboration in the late 1970s and early 1980s of a 'new' realism (Keohane 1986), purporting to offer a more theoretically rigorous version of classical realism. 'Neorealists' (or, more correctly, structural realists) argued that world politics could be best understood by its structure. In this version of realism, states were led to dominate others by the anarchic structure of the system in which they found themselves. Structural realists like Waltz (1979) and Walt (1986) argued that the only way to avoid domination by others was by seeking power, either singly or in combination with other states. The apogee of this view of the impact of structure was reflected in the theory of 'offensive' realism, which asserts that every great power is forced by the nature of the system, as Mearsheimer (2001, 29) put it, to search 'for opportunities to gain power over their rivals, with hegemony as their final goal'.

In turn, neorealism (or structural realism) and offensive realism spawned the emergence of a neoclassical realist school that argued that the structure of the system, while important, does not necessarily have such overweening deterministic power. Rather, other factors, such as perception and misperception of others, a country's domestic politics, including the capacity of state leaders to mobilize a state's power or generate domestic support, all contribute to a state's foreign policy behavior (for example, Rose 1998).

For all their differences, however, what unites the strands of realist thought is the belief in the atomistic existence of states – even if they do exist in a 'social' context, as English School scholars suggest; the importance of selfishness based on materialist conceptions of interest; and the importance of power to advance those interests.

While the tenets of realism are continually challenged by alternative theoretical approaches, it is important to recognize the degree to which the tenets of realist thought remain strongly entrenched, not only in the academy, but also in policy circles. Consider the perspective of H.R. McMaster, the U.S. National Security Advisor in the administration of Donald J. Trump, and Gary D. Cohn, Trump's chief economic adviser. In an op-ed written after Trump's first foreign trip in May 2017, they wrote that the president had:

> a clear-eyed outlook that the world is not a 'global community' but an arena where nations, nongovernmental actors and businesses engage and compete for advantage... Rather than deny this elemental nature of international affairs, we embrace it (McMaster and Cohn 2017).

Needless to say, an interest-based, atomistic view of world politics will have important implications for how one understands how foreign policy is made, how alliances and coalitions work, why states will intervene in some conflicts and not in others, and whether non-material factors will shape foreign policy outcomes. Fouad Ajami put the interest-based argument succinctly in his response to Huntington's 1993 article: 'States avert their gaze from blood ties when they need to; they see brotherhood and faith and kin when it is in their interest to do so'. He went on to remind us of the lessons of the Melian dialogue:

> Besieged by Athens, [the Melians] held out and were sure that the Lacedaemonians were 'bound, if only for very shame, to come to the aid of their kindred'. The Melians never wavered in their confidence in their 'civilizational' allies: 'Our common blood insures our fidelity.' We know what became of the Melians. Their allies did not turn up, their island was sacked, their world laid to waste (Ajami 1993, 9).

The problem with the orthodox realist theories of international relations, however, is that they cannot account for those international relationships that are patently *not* marked by the atomism and selfishness predicted by the orthodox theory. For there are a number of international relationships where there is a rather different political dynamic at work, one that does not conform to the predictions of any of the realist perspectives. On the contrary: in some international relationships, ties of 'sentiment' – in other words, kinship – must form much of the explanation for the relationships of these countries (and indeed their governments and peoples). These are not atomistic units, always seeking self-interest pure and simple, with outcomes determined by power differentials. Rather, they are linked by ties of different sorts: economic, commercial, familial, political, diplomatic, strategic, language, and culture. And power, when it is exercised, tends to be exercised in a less brutal fashion than predicted by realist theory.

Importantly, there is an 'insider' element that comes with such shared attributes as language, culture, institutions, and history that provide crucial commonalities for peoples of different and independent political communities. Such shared attributes provide the basis for widely shared cultural understandings that tend not be present when such critical elements are absent. In short, there are some international relationships that simply cannot be understood through a realist lens.

One could point to the former communities of the British Empire – Australia, Canada, New Zealand, the United States, and post-imperial Britain itself – as prototypical kin-countries. The relationships between and among these five countries are fundamentally different than relations among most other states, and certainly do not conform to the way that realists describe and explain international relations.

First, there is a sense of commonality, shared identity – the 'we-feeling' identified by Deutsch (1957) that is so necessary for the establishment of a security community (Adler and Barnett 1998). To be sure, that shared identity is stronger in some cases than others: the strong 'we-feeling' across the Tasman Sea between Australia and New Zealand does not compare, for example, to feelings between Americans and Australians. But there can be little doubt that in all five communities, there is a sense of exceptionalism that means, for example, that the use of force between these countries as a means of securing national objectives has become unthinkable. In this, these five countries constitute an unambiguous security community (Adler and Barnett 1998) that is also a zone of democratic peace (Roussel 2004); their relationships among each other exhibit the dynamics predicted in cases of complex interdependence (Keohane and Nye 1977).

Second, there is a deep culture of interconnectedness between these communities. These connections are not just driven by material factors such as trade and investment, but in people-to-people links between families, students, and tourism. Of particular importance are the connections at the transgovernmental level that we simply do not see in many other international contexts (Fox, Hero and Nye 1976; Thompson and Randall, 2008). Relations are marked by a complex institutionalization that binds these separate and independent communities. The Five Eyes (FVEY) intelligence alliance is one manifestation of that close relationship. The ease with which government officials are exchanged in some of these dyads (in particular Australia-New Zealand, Australia-Canada) is another. Likewise, the willingness of the United States to give the command of units of its armed forces to Canadian officers on secondment speaks to a culture of closeness that is not to be found in other dyadic relationships.

Third, there are strong links that manifest themselves in military terms. In a historical context, the kin-country relationships of some of these dyads featured that most basic feature of kinship in a social context: the willingness of members of one political community to put themselves in harm's way to protect the interests of another community. Consider the case of Australia, Canada and New Zealand during the Imperial era. Australians, Canadians and New Zealanders fought in the Boer War in 1899, and in 1914, by which time all three countries were self-governing dominions within the British Empire. Hundreds of thousands of Australians, Canadians and New Zealanders were willing to put themselves in harm's way in defence of a wider political community (Nossal 2004).

While in a post-Imperial context there is little that remains of those earlier sentiments – during the Falklands/Malvinas War of 1982, for example, none of the former dominions offered to assist Britain in its war against Argentina – there is nonetheless a continued willingness to commit the nation's resources to the defence and assistance to a cause that might be objectively 'foreign' and 'alien', but which one believes to be (or constructs as being) one's own, and hence in one's self-interest. Thus, for example, Australia and New Zealand both contributed troops to the American war in Vietnam in the 1960s. And Australia, Britain, Canada and New Zealand all responded by sending troops to Afghanistan after the attack on the United States on 11 September 2001.

One small, but telling, indication of the nature of the relationship has been the tendency to use the language of family to describe others in the community. In the Imperial era, for example, it was common for Australians, Canadians and New Zealanders to refer to Britain in national discourse as the 'mother country'. Today, 'cousins' tends to be the preferred familial metaphor (Patten 2006; Blaxland 2006), though the language of family and kin continues to be used in official discourse. For example, when Donald J. Trump met Theresa May, the British prime minister, on 27 January 2017, he began his remarks by noting his own family connection to the United Kingdom; and May, for her part, noted that the US-UK relationship was 'based on the bonds of history, of family, kinship and common interests' (White House 2017).

But to what extent are these kin-countries connected to Huntingtonesque civilizations? The analysis above suggests that civilization – as defined by Huntington – has very little to do with the kinship ties between these five countries. To be sure, they are all part of the 'West', as broadly defined by Huntington, but the particular kinship links that continue to bind Australia, Britain, Canada, New Zealand and the United States together cannot be explained in the kind of 'civilizational' terms that Huntington uses.

On the contrary: as Srdjan Vucetic (2011) has shown, the construction of a larger 'kin-country' community between these countries was racial rather than civilizational. The key, he argues, was the idea of an 'Anglo-Saxon' *race* that identified a commonality between Britain and its 'white dominions' (in order of seniority, Canada, Australia, and New Zealand) on the one hand and the United States on the other that was racial, even though it was often referred to in linguistic terms by such enthusiasts as Winston S. Churchill as the 'English-speaking peoples'. To be sure, that definition of 'race' did not mirror objective reality: there were French-speaking Canadians; indigenous peoples in Australia, Canada, New Zealand and the United States; a 'Celtic fringe' (Vucetic 2011, 28) in the United Kingdom (and Australia); and, in the United States, a large African-American population and a Hispanic population that grew over the course of the twentieth century. But as Vucetic shows, constructions of Anglo-Saxonism in the late nineteenth and early twentieth centuries finessed and marginalized these groups. Instead, the 'race patriotism' (Vucetic 2011, 29) of the era stressed the superiority of Anglo-Saxons over others. Indeed, what British leaders, such as Arthur Balfour and Joseph Chamberlain, openly called a 'race alliance' lay behind the rapprochement between the British Empire and the United States at the turn of twentieth century. And this, in a path-dependent way, set the stage for the consolidation of a security community between countries that evolved in the post-Imperial (but not post-imperial) order of the twentieth century, a security community that continues in the twenty-first century.

Importantly, this racialized construction of Anglo-Saxonism, bounded as it was with a linguistic fence, was purposely designed to exclude others who might nonetheless have been part of a broader Western civilization. The 'West' as a Huntingtonian civilizational group might have grown from the British-American rapprochement and the Entente Cordiale across the English Channel in the early twentieth century to the expansion of both NATO and the European Union after the collapse of the Soviet Union at century's end, but the kind of kin-country relations that developed between the United States, Britain and the three former dominions never developed with any other countries within the Western alliance.

Moreover, it is clear that the kin-country relationship that developed between these countries is a *cas unique* in contemporary global politics. While we can find patterns of friendship between countries developed on numerous bases – language (*la Francophonie*, *Cumbre Iberoamericana,* for example), religion (Organization of Islamic Cooperation), or even former colonial membership (the Commonwealth or *La Francophonie*) – there simply is no comparable grouping of states that have the same kind of relationship as these five countries.

Conclusion

I have argued that Huntington was right to call attention to the phenomenon of kin-countries. To be sure, most students of international relations and foreign policy in the smaller kin-countries explored in this chapter were already aware of the phenomenon, even if, like Molière's Monsieur Jourdain, they were not using the language of kin-country in their scholarship. But they fully understood that there are certain international relationships that are simply not well explained by orthodox international relations theorizing, particularly not realist theories.

But, paradoxically, the idea of kin-country can only be made useful if it is stripped of its 'clash of civilizations' baggage. In other words, looking at some international relationships through the lens of a sense of kinship – whether defined, as Vucetic does, as a racialized identity, or focusing on attributes such as politico-strategic or economic interests, language, common historical origins or political institutions, culture, religion, or 'way of life' – makes considerably more sense than trying to understand those relationships using the precepts of realism. But those kinship ties, it is clear, have little to do with 'civilization', as Huntington was using the term. Likewise, the 'rallying' that was so central to Huntington's conception of kin-country is not only problematic more generally – as widely noted by critics – but makes no appearance in the relationships of the kin-countries looked at in this chapter.

In short, the concept of kin-country remains too closely identified with Huntington's broader civilizational argument to be able to enjoy anything but a tadpole existence, and certainly will never be able to develop autonomously from the project that spawned it 25 years ago. Kin-country seems doomed to be an analytical category that is useful but, sadly, unusable.

References

Adler, Emmanuel, and Michael Barnett, eds. 1998. *Security Communities*. Cambridge: Cambridge University Press.

Ajami, Fouad. 1993. "The Summoning: 'But They Said, We Will Not Hearken.'" *Foreign Affairs* 72(4): 2–9.

Betts, Richard K. 2010. "Conflict or Cooperation? Three Visions Revisited." *Foreign Affairs* 89(6): 186–94.

Blaxland, John C. 2006. *Strategic Cousins: Australian and Canadian Expeditionary Forces and the British and American Empires*. Montréal and Kingston: McGill-Queen's University Press.

Bull, Hedley. 1977. *The Anarchical Society: A Study of Order in World Politics*. New York: Columbia University Press.

Deutsch, Karl. 1957. *Political Community and the North Atlantic Area*. Princeton: Princeton University Press.

Fox, Annette Baker, Alfred O. Hero, Jr., and Joseph S. Nye, eds. 1976. *Canada and the United States: Transnational and Transgovernmental Relations*. New York: Columbia University Press.

Greenway, H.D.S. 1992. "The Kin-Country Syndrome is Adding to the Crisis in Bosnia." *Boston Globe*, 3 December.

Huntington, Samuel P. 1993. "The Clash of Civilizations?" *Foreign Affairs* 72(3): 22–49.

Huntington, Samuel P. 1993. "If Not Civilizations, What? Samuel Huntington Responds to His Critics." *Foreign Affairs* 72(5). https://www.foreignaffairs.com/articles/global-commons/1993-12-01/if-not-civilizations-what-samuel-huntington-responds-his-critics Accessed 02 December 2017.

Huntington, Samuel P. 1996. *The Clash of Civilizations and the Remaking of World Order*. New York: Simon & Schuster.

Keohane, Robert O. and Joseph S. Nye, Jr. 1977. *Power and Interdependence: World Politics in Transition*. Boston: Little, Brown and Company.

McMaster, H.R. and Gary D. Cohn. 2017. "America First Doesn't Mean America Alone." *Wall Street Journal*, 31 May.

Mearsheimer, John. 2001. *The Tragedy of Great Power Politics*. New York: Norton.

Morgenthau, Hans J. 1948. *Politics Among Nations: The Struggle for Power and Peace*. New York: Alfred A. Knopf.

Morgenthau, Hans J. 2005. *Politics Among Nations: The Struggle for Power and Peace*, 7th Rev. Ed. by Kenneth Thompson, and W. David Clinton. New York: McGraw Hill Education

Nossal, Kim Richard. 2004. "Defending the 'Realm': Canadian Strategic Culture Revisited." *International Journal* 59(3): 503–20.

Patten, Chris. 2006. *Cousins and Strangers: America, Britain, and Europe in a New Century*. New York: Henry Holt and Company.

Peletz, Michael G. 1995. "Kinship Studies in Late Twentieth-Century Anthropology." *Annual Review of Anthropology* 24(1): 343–72.

Rose, Gideon. 1998. "Neoclassical Realism and Theories of Foreign Policy." *World Politics* 51(1): 144–72.

Roussel, Stéphane. 2004. *The North American Democratic Peace: Absence of War and Security Institution-Building in Canada-US Relations, 1867–1958.* Montréal and Kingston: McGill-Queen's University Press.

Rubenstein, Richard E., and Jarle Crocker. 1994. "Challenging Huntington." *Foreign Policy* 9(96): 113–28.

Thompson, John Herd, and Stephen J. Randall. 2008. *Canada and the United States: Ambivalent Allies*, 4th ed. Montréal and Kingston: McGill-Queen's University Press.

Vucetic, Srdjan. 2011. *The Anglosphere: A Genealogy of a Racialized Identity in International Relations*. Stanford: Stanford University Press.

Walt, Stephen. 1986. *The Origins of Alliances*. Ithaca: Cornell University Press.

Waltz, Kenneth N. 1979. *Theory of International Politics*. Reading, Mass.: Addison Wesley.

The White House. 2017. "President Trump and Prime Minister May's Opening Remarks." *Office of the Press Secretary*, 27 January. https://www.whitehouse.gov/the-press-office/2017/01/27/president-trump-and-prime-minister-mays-opening-remarks Accessed 30 November 2017.

7

Huntington vs. Mearsheimer vs. Fukuyama: Which Post-Cold War Thesis is Most Accurate?

GLEN M.E. DUERR

In the aftermath of the Cold War – a 45-year ideological struggle between the United States and the Soviet Union – several scholars forecasted the future of conflict and geopolitics post-1991. Three prominent books – Samuel Huntington's *The Clash of Civilizations*, John Mearsheimer's *The Tragedy of Great Power Politics*, and Francis Fukuyama's *The End of History*, all with compelling theses, provide a roadmap as to possible future outcomes. These three books have been selected, in part, because Huntington actually criticizes the main theories of the two others authors in Chapter one of his book, *The Clash of Civilizations and the Remaking of World Order* (Huntington 1997, 31, 37).

Francis Fukuyama's book, *The End of History and the Last Man*, outlines the success of democracy and free-market capitalism as the dominant ideology that would proliferate throughout the world after the dissolution of the Soviet Union, and the representative death of communism as a viable ideological position (Fukuyama 1992). In a sense, warfare in the post-Cold War is unlikely given the rise of democracy and interdependence, Fukuyama argues. Since democracy is the final form of human government, debating Karl Marx's admonition that communism would replace capitalism; Fukuyama effectively argues the opposite of Marx that capitalism has triumphed. Fukuyama also argues that although democracy is not a panacea to cure all problems of humanity, it is the final form of government.

John Mearsheimer's book, *The Tragedy of Great Power Politics*, provides an overview of the international system from a structural realist (also known as a neo-realist) perspective, specifically offensive realism. In contrast to early classical realist scholars like Hans Morgenthau, Mearsheimer argues that the structure of the international system is a cause of war, not necessarily moral concerns, or the particular characteristics of a given leader. In contrast to other structural realists like Kenneth Waltz, Mearsheimer argues that – on the questions of how much power states want to accumulate – states want as much power as they can get, rather than what he terms defensive realists who contend that states are interested in maintaining the balance of power (Mearsheimer 2001, 22).

Mearsheimer's core predictions circulate around the changing dynamics in geopolitics as related to 'great powers'. Mearsheimer argues that conflict is a fact of the international system because ultimately the dynamics of great power politics lead to wars over dominance of the system. Mearsheimer's book concentrates on an almost 200-year period from the start of the Napoleonic Wars, 1792, to the end of the Cold War, 1991. He argues that three central wars occurred – the Napoleonic Wars, World War I, and World War II – when the international system of balance of power politics was both unbalanced and multipolar (Mearsheimer 2001, 357). Thus, even though Mearsheimer does not directly discuss the post-Cold War world, his theory provides predictive power as to what will happen in the future based on characteristics that, he argues, have held over time. In the post-Cold War world, other 'great powers', given enough time, will seek to balance the power of the United States. The world is particularly conflict-prone when a multi-polar world arises, especially if the balance-of-power becomes unbalanced (Mearsheimer 2001). Thus, when Mearsheimer published his book in 2001, the US was clearly the only superpower in the world.

Finally, Samuel P. Huntington's 'clash of civilizations' article in *Foreign Affairs* spawned such furious debate in 1993 that Huntington published a full-length book in 1996 to assuage his critics (Huntington 1993; Huntington 1997). Revolving around nine civilizations, Huntington argues that the future of warfare would be fought along civilizational 'fault lines'. The civilizations include the West, Latin America, Africa, Orthodox, Sinic, Islamic, Hindu, Buddhist and Japanese. From the 1993 article to the 1996 book, Huntington added Japanese as a separate civilization, and changed Confucian to Sinic. One of the most controversial components of Huntington's argument is the line 'Islam has bloody borders' (Huntington 1993, 35) inferring that the Islamic civilization in particular tends to become violently embroiled with other civilizations on its periphery. The case here is based on wars such as the Yugoslav war, conflict in Sudan and Iraq, as well as the Philippines.

Each thesis provides compelling reasons as to the future of the world, especially during the post-Cold War period. Huntington and Mearsheimer, in particular, utilize a theoretical argument in order to provide a forecast of the future. This is the major upside of using an accepted theory because it allows for predictions despite the fact that no scholar can readily predict what will actually happen. As John Mearsheimer is fond of saying, 'the leaders of tomorrow are in the fifth grade today, and we have no way of predicting how they will act. But, theory provides us with a framework of their expected behaviors'.[1]

Now that an overview of each scholar's major post-Cold War thesis has been presented, this chapter will first assess the arguments of Fukuyama and Mearsheimer as to their predictive power. Which topics and events has each author correctly predicted, and which topics and events has each author missed; in essence, which theory is most accurate? Given that this volume is an assessment of the work of Samuel Huntington, special attention is paid to the 'clash of civilizations' thesis in the latter half of the chapter, but always with a comparison of Fukuyama and Mearsheimer in the background. Ultimately, I argue that each scholars' prediction has, at periods of time in the post-Cold War era, looked very strong, whilst, at other times, their predictions have either not come to fruition, or been incorrect. Each thesis is still salvageable, but democracy is currently on the decline, which undercuts Fukuyama; great power competition has still not really emerged, which undercuts Mearsheimer; and civilizational identity remains limited, which undercuts Huntington. For each scholar, however, is known for their comprehensive grasp of history, so their work should be assessed regularly to see if their predictions correctly prognosticated events in the long term.

Which Theory is Most Accurate?

At various points since the formal end of the Cold War in 1991, each of the scholars' predictions has looked at times like a successful explanation of the current era, but also, at other times, like respective theses that missed the central explanatory factors of the period – prognosticating after all is a very difficult endeavor. Fukuyama's thesis looked strong throughout the 1990s with the proliferation of democracies and states adopting free-market principles, even with requisite state protections (perhaps best called mixed economies). However, with 9/11, and wars in Afghanistan and Iraq, Huntington's 'clash of civilizations' theory began to take hold as a better explanation of why geopolitical actions happened the way they did. Moreover, with the rise of China, and the resurgence of Russia – both utilizing an illiberal model of governance – Fukuyama's thesis was likewise challenged by Mearsheimer's

---

[1]   Mearsheimer made this statement at the 2013 International Studies Association conference in San Francisco, California, on a panel discussion.

prediction that other states would attempt to balance the power of the hegemon. Despite the challenges, parts of Fukuyama's thesis still hold in that democracy remains an appealing force in world politics. Even though democracy has declined for the eleventh straight year, 87 of the 195 measured countries are still labelled as 'free' (Freedom House 2017). Tangentially, Fukuyama's work also buttresses the Democratic Peace Theory (DPT), which layers his prediction with a Churchillian argument that democracy is the best form of government despite its flaws. Although Fukuyama did not construct the DPT, his positions on democracy strengthened the DPT by emphasizing the importance of democracy as the final form of human government. The DPT still holds if democracy and war are given strict definitions, and if intrastate conflicts are omitted. These two points show that Fukuyama's *End of History* thesis is at the very least still relevant today.

For Fukuyama, democracy is central. The DPT posits that mature democracies do not go to war with other mature democracies (see Doyle 1986; Doyle 2005). The monadic version of the theory – assessing whether or not democracies are peaceful or not compared to non-democracies – is the argument that, yes, democracies are generally more peaceful than any other type of regime. For the monadic theory, the actual evidence however is at best mixed since democratic countries like the United States and the United Kingdom still frequently go to war against non-democracies. However, some evidence exists as to support the dyadic version of the theory – assessing whether *mature* democracies are more peaceful when surveying their likelihood of going to war against other *mature* democracies – that, yes, democracies do not really go to war with each other. In general, the dyadic version of the DPT is upheld statistically, and in the academic literature. Depending on how democracy and war are defined, it is possible to argue that the DPT has held from the end of the Napoleonic Wars in 1815 to the present – a span of over 200 years. There are numerous cases that might upend this thesis, but if a democracy is defined as a mature democracy replete with robust democratic institutions, and a history of competitive elections. If war is defined as 1,000 battle-related deaths per year, rather than 25. Finally, if civil wars, or intrastate wars, are omitted, then the veracity of the dyadic version of the DPT might still hold. Fukuyama's adherence to democracy buttresses the concept that mature democracies are the final form of government due to a range of social goods for the people, but also in minimizing interstate violence in the future.

What undercuts Fukuyama's thesis, however, is the stubbornness of China to reform even with significant per capita economic growth; Russia's backsliding into authoritarianism under President Vladimir Putin; Turkey's authoritarianism under President Recep Erdoğan; and numerous strongmen that have emerged even since 2010 such as President al-Sisi of Egypt. In a sense, the

2010s have been dominated by an authoritarian resurgence where the strongman figure is seen as necessary in order to provide stability in a tumultuous economic and security environment around the world. In 2008, Fukuyama defended his thesis arguing that while autocracy has increased, especially in the aftermath of Russia's invasion of Georgia, authoritarian leaders can only go so far – 'If today's autocrats are willing to bow to democracy, they are eager to grovel to capitalism' (Fukuyama 2008). In his op-ed in *The Washington Post*, Fukuyama concedes that democracy is not necessarily the end of history given the rise of Islamic fundamentalism, but he argues that this challenge may subside or be defeated.

The work of John Mearsheimer is still largely untested for two main reasons. First, because US power remains central to security discussions in Europe – his theory rests on a return to great power rivalry in Europe, which, he argues, would return if the United States vacated its troops from the continent. Second, because the US remains the sole superpower, even if great power rivals are emerging elsewhere in the world, no country can balance American power, thus an unbalanced multipolar world is impossible. On the first point, Germany has not yet developed the requisite strategic autonomy to become a military superpower, which is well within Berlin's arsenal should it pursue a more muscular foreign policy if latent tensions with the US continue to develop. For example, schisms between President George W. Bush and Chancellor Gerhard Schroeder, and their contemporaries Trump and Merkel suggest that this division is possible. Mearsheimer cannot claim credit yet because the world remains devoid of great power conflict. Inter-dependence and cooperation still prevail and have disrupted the challenges that Mearsheimer predicted with rising multipolarity in the state system.

Mearsheimer also argues (2006) that given the Thucydidean trap of international relations – that one power cannot rise without coming into conflict with the falling power – China and the US will engage in some form of confrontation in the future. He ultimately argues that the US will treat China much the same as it did the Soviet Union during the Cold War with a policy of containment, and defeat China if Washington pursues smart policies. Multipolarity takes time to emerge, but with the rise of the Chinese economy coupled with technological improvements to their military, Beijing has emerged as a superpower for some academics, pundits, and policymakers. Russia's military actions in Georgia in 2008, Ukraine in 2014, and Syria in 2015 suggest that Moscow may be a resurgent actor in world affairs, worthy of great power status. There is some evidence of emerging multipolarity, then, with China, Russia, and other major actors like India. Questions, however, remain on the actions of Germany and Japan – both of which should emerge as 'great powers' under Mearsheimer's model. Thus, Mearsheimer's theory is still largely untested because the correct conditions of unbalanced multipolarity have not yet emerged.

Huntington Debates Mearsheimer and Fukuyama

Interestingly, as noted in the introduction, Huntington specifically criticizes the theories of Fukuyama and Mearsheimer in Chapter one of his book because they both provide contrasting visions of the post-Cold War world. In a sense, Fukuyama's thesis is one of harmony in the post-Cold War world – a point that Huntington vigorously views as overly optimistic and unlikely – because, in Fukuyama's view, there would be no major struggles over ideology in the future such as those that preceded World War I, World War II, and the Cold War (Huntington, 1997, 31). Fukuyama concedes that conflicts would still take place in the "Third World" (now usually called the developing world), but that the end of history marks 'the end point of mankind's ideological evolution and the universalization of Western liberal democracy as the final form of human government' (Huntington, 1997, 31).

Assessed from the vantage point of 2018, 25 years after his initial prediction, Huntington is certainly right in his pessimism of Fukuyama's thesis, at least to some degree. Fukuyama's thesis has not delivered the universalization of Western liberal democracy, and has eroded since its high point in 2010. However, unlike World War I with monarchism, World War II with fascism and the Cold War with communism (see Mazower 1999), the post-Cold War world does not have one, distinct ideology with which capitalism and liberal democracy are competing. Fukuyama therefore cannot be easily dismissed, especially if the backsliding of democracy in the 2010s is merely a blip on a wider trend towards democratization, and if there is no major competitor for liberal democracy. Perhaps the rise of authoritarian state-centric capitalism in China and Russia provides an alternate ideological model for post-Cold War conflict, but democratic variants in Japan and South Korea still show that democratization is highly prized in tangent with a state-driven form of capitalism.

Huntington also criticizes Mearsheimer, specifically over his predictions on Russia and Ukraine, although he makes two contradictory claims. First, Mearsheimer predicts that 'the situation between Ukraine and Russia is ripe for the outbreak of security competition between them. For a great power like Russia that shares a long and unprotected common border, like the one between Russia and Ukraine, often lapse into competition driven by security fears. Russia and Ukraine might overcome this dynamic and learn to live in harmony, but it would be unusual if they do' (Mearsheimer 1993, 54 cited in Huntington 1996, 37). Huntington refutes this argument and instead argues that a civilizational approach is a better explanation of the peace between the two countries because they share the same civilizational culture – thus, peace is the more likely outcome. However, in a later section of Huntington's book, the second point he makes on Ukraine/Russia, is that he describes Ukraine as a 'cleft country', which is torn, in a sense, between two civilizations (Huntington 1997, 166). 'A civilizational approach', Huntington argues that it, 'highlights the possibility of Ukraine splitting in half, a separation which cultural factors would lead one to predict might be more violent than that of Czechoslovakia but far less bloody than Yugoslavia' (Huntington 1997, 37).

When viewing the world in 2018, 25 years after the publication of *The Clash of Civilizations*, Mearsheimer's thesis certainly looks better than Huntington's given Russia's annexation of Crimea in 2014, and the interjection of covert Russian forces in the Eastern Ukrainian regions of Donetsk and Luhansk. Huntington is still correct in his assessment that a split of Ukraine would be bloodier than Czechoslovakia, but less so then Yugoslavia, but incorrectly diagnosed Mearsheimer's state-centric argument that Russia and Ukraine would likely engage in some form of violent war over security concerns, rather than civilizational kinship. Against Mearsheimer, Huntington's thesis is certainly less accurate in some places. Mearsheimer correctly predicts the likelihood of violence between Russia and Ukraine, something that Huntington dismisses because he assumed that civilizational identity would become paramount, rather than the security-based rivalry that Mearsheimer asserts. Huntington's discussion of Ukraine as a 'cleft country' revitalizes his argument because it implicitly notes the possibility that Ukraine would splinter – a bold prediction to make when assessing any country. Moreover, Huntington's assessment that Ukraine would split in a manner more violent than Czechoslovakia, but less violent than Yugoslavia, is currently correct. Mearsheimer thus holds some leverage over Huntington on this issue, but the depth and specificity of Huntington's predictions purport his sophisticated foresight.

9/11, the Afghan and Iraq wars, the Failure of the Arab Spring, and the Rise of ISIS

Turning specifically to Huntington for the remainder of the chapter, what are the successes of his argument? Huntington's thesis presents some explanation of 9/11, the failure of the Arab Spring, the rise of ISIS, and the threat of terrorism especially in the West. Yet, at the same time, inter-civilizational fault lines have not produced mass conflict. Civil wars are relatively rare even in places where civilizations meet (see Goldstein, 2011). Parts of Huntington's thesis hold in the measures noted above, but his explanation should have generated more conflict, and less cross-civilizational cooperation such as the rise of BRICS, and the inter-civilizational coalition to defeat ISIS.

Where has Huntington been successful? In his book, Huntington provides 19 bullet points (Huntington, 1997, 38-39) that show how the post-Cold War world is moving towards a civilizational approach. Since the publication of his book, there are certainly many more bullet points that could be added. However, four major events fall categorically successful for Huntington's prediction. As noted in the above section, Huntington's theory showed significant accuracy in 2001 with 9/11 – if Huntington's clashing civilizations thesis had been taken more seriously, some argue, the US could have better prepared for a 9/11-type event. In the aftermath of 9/11, the wars on Afghanistan and Iraq also provide some justification for Huntington.

The war on Afghanistan received widespread support and NATO's triggering of Article V – Huntington predicted the concept of civilizational kin rallying, especially in times of war or major attack. The Iraq War was much more contentious, and, in some senses, caused inter-civilizational disagreements since France, Germany, and Canada, among others in the West opposed the invasion of Iraq, all trying to offset the 'clash of civilizations' thesis by not aligning with the wider Western civilization. This cuts against Huntington's thesis to some degree, but the waging of war by a country from one civilization (the West) against another (Islamic) bolsters the original 'clash of civilizations' thesis.

At the outset of the Arab Spring when Mohamed Bouazizi self-immolated in Tunisia in December 2010, it kick-started a chain of protests across the Middle East and North Africa (MENA). When President Ben Ali of Tunisia was ousted followed in quick succession by President Mubarak of Egypt in January 2011 and then President Gadhafi of Libya in the midst of a bloody civil war, it seemed like the MENA region – the last vestige of widespread autocracy – might begin the process of democratization. The President of Yemen Ali Abdullah Saleh also resigned, and liberal reforms took hold in Morocco, Kuwait, and Jordan among other cases. Fukuyama's thesis recovered somewhat in 2011 and 2012 despite the downturn of democracy elsewhere in the world.

However, as protests in Syria beginning in March of 2011 segued into a fissiparous civil war, the early optimism of the Arab Spring began to wane, before finally petering out. Democratic successes are still evident in some MENA societies, and further reforms may still be enacted, but at least for now, the Arab Spring movement has subsided. Huntington's 'clash of civilizations' theory did not predict the short-term failure of the Arab Spring. However, he did predict that Islam would be the prominent defining feature of the MENA region as an Islamic civilization controversially implying that some of the values would be anathema to values in other civilizations such as democracy in the West.

The rise of ISIS as a significant player in the conflicts in the Middle East, especially in Syria and Iraq, but also in Yemen and Libya, does not necessarily uphold Huntington's thesis, but provides some suggestion of Huntington's prediction. Since Huntington (1997) divided the world into nine different civilizations including an Islamic civilization, the goal of ISIS is to unify this civilization under a radical Islamist banner. Huntington is incorrect in the sense that a majority of people in the Middle East and North Africa still reject the ISIS-vision of a radical form of sharia law, but Huntington argues that Islam will be the key defining feature of the civilization. At this point, Huntington's thesis still holds since a group like ISIS rose to prominence.

A global war involving core states of the world's major civilizations is highly improbable but not impossible. Such a war, we have suggested, could come about from the escalation of a fault line was between groups from different civilizations, most likely involving Muslims on one side and non-Muslims on the other (Huntington 1997, 312).

On one of Huntington's most controversial points, 'Islam has bloody borders' the rise of ISIS suggests some accuracy on the part of Huntington given the deadliness of this group. Missed in the wider narrative, however, is the prevailing peace in the world. The political scientist, Joshua Goldstein, shows that interstate war has declined dramatically such that in some years, there were no interstate wars at any place in the world (Goldstein 2011). Although conflict has increased since 2011, interstate violence remains relatively rare. Thus, Huntington's assertion that 'Islam has bloody borders' is on one level true, it ignores the decline of violence everywhere. Based on Huntington's prediction, one would actually expect a lot more violence in places where the Islamic civilization meets other civilizations, and yet political violence, and both interstate and intrastate wars remain relatively low compared to other points in human history.

Overall, on all four points, and despite some shortcomings, Huntington remains relevant to the post-Cold War debate. At the end of his book, Samuel Huntington openly wrestled with the idea of a clear civilizational identity. He argues, for example, that the United States should reject multiculturalism in order to preserve its place in the Western civilization,

The futures of the United States and of the West depend upon Americans reaffirming their commitment to Western civilization. Domestically this means rejecting the divisive siren calls of multiculturalism. Internationally it means rejecting the elusive and illusory calls to identify the United States with Asia (Huntington 1997, 307).

There is a portion of the above quote that suggests Huntington predicted the rise of an American presidential candidate like President Donald Trump – someone with an America First type disposition that is generally viewed as more nationalistic than previous presidents. Trump's success, in some ways, is due to a Huntingtonian admonition to rally around one's civilization (see Huntington 2004), one that President Trump has thus far fulfilled given his disdain for globalization, and his desire to reduce illegal immigration especially from civilizations outside of the West. Although there are some clear distinctions, President Trump's rhetoric and actions mirror some of the three sentences listed above as important by Huntington to maintain the United States' role as leader of the West. Huntington's work was very controversial when first published in 1993 leading to a vociferous debate in the pages of *Foreign Affairs* and elsewhere. When viewing the world in 2018, Huntington is no less controversial, but also still seems to speak to the present. As a means of testing whether his thesis still holds intellectual ground 25 years later, the mere fact that Huntingtonian assessments are still relevant in the 2016 and 2020 US Presidential Election debates, shows an answer in the affirmative. The same critiques of Huntington being too broad, not specific enough in some areas, and conceding some ground to his intellectual rivals exemplified by Fukuyama and Mearsheimer, all remain. Nevertheless, scholars cannot discount Huntington because core parts of his arguments still remain relevant to the narratives of today even if Huntington is clearly incorrect in some places.

* *The author would like to thank Jacob Mach for his help with researching content for this chapter. The original idea for this chapter comes from Dr. Andrew Barnes and Dr. Steven Hook of Kent State University.*

References

Doyle, Michael W. 1986. "Liberalism and world politics." *American Political Science Review* 80(4): 1151–1169.

Doyle, Michael W. 2005. "Three pillars of the liberal peace." *American Political Science Review* 99(3): 463–466.

Freedom House. 2017. "Populists and Autocrats: The Dual Threat to Global Democracy." https://freedomhouse.org/report/freedom-world/freedom-world-2017 Accessed 15 February 2017.

Fukuyama, Francis. 1989. "The End of History?." *The National Interest* 16: 3–18.

Fukuyama, Francis. 1992. *The End of History and the Last Man*. New York: Simon and Schuster.

Fukuyama, Francis. 2008. "They can only go so far." *Washington Post*, 24 August. http://www.washingtonpost.com/wpdyn/content/article/2008/08/22/AR2008082202395.html Accessed 22 June 2017.

Goldstein, Joshua S. 2011. *Winning the War on War: The Decline of Armed Conflict Worldwide*. New York: Penguin.

Huntington, Samuel P. 1993. "The Clash of Civilizations?" *Foreign Affairs* 72(3): 22–49.

Huntington, Samuel P. 1997. *The Clash of Civilizations and the Remaking of World Order*. New York: Simon & Schuster.

Huntington, Samuel P. 1999. "The lonely superpower." *Foreign Affairs* 78(2): 35–49.

Huntington, Samuel P. 2004. *Who are we?: The challenges to America's national identity*. New York: Simon and Schuster.

Mazower, Mark 2000. *Dark Continent: Europe's Twentieth Century*. New York: Vintage Books.

Mearsheimer, John. 1993. "The case for a Ukrainian nuclear deterrent." *Foreign Affairs* 72(3): 50–66.

Mearsheimer, John. 1990. "Back to the Future: Instability in Europe After the Cold War." *International Security* 15(1): 5–56.

Mearsheimer, John. 2001. *The Tragedy of Great Power Politics*. New York: WW Norton & Company.

Mearsheimer, John. 2006. "China's Unpeaceful Rise." *Current History* 105(690): 160–162.

8

Plus ça Change… Civilizations, Political Systems and Power Politics: A Critique of Huntington's 'Clash of Civilizations'

ANNA KHAKEE

In an article – and later a book – that have received more attention than perhaps any others in International Relations, Samuel P. Huntington predicted that the 'West and the rest' would clash because of differences in religion and civilization as the 'highest cultural grouping of people and the broadest level of cultural identity people have' (Huntington 1993, 24). Huntington's hypothesis was that 'the fault lines between civilizations' would replace Cold War ideological boundaries as the 'flash points for crisis and bloodshed' (Huntington 1993, 29; Huntington 1996, 125).

Over the 25 years since its first publication, Huntington's essays have been widely discussed and roundly criticized from a variety of perspectives. Indeed, it would probably be fair to say that while 'The Clash of Civilizations?' made Huntington (1993) more of a household name that that of any other political scientist, it at the same time reduced his – previously stellar – standing in scholarly circles. Peers have found fault with its logic, consistency and strong tendency to simplify complex phenomena (Bottici and Challand 2006), perfunctory treatment of empirical case studies (Ajami 1993), lack of backing by empirical statistical evidence (Russett et al 2000; Henderson and Tucker 2001; Fox 2001), confounding political and social conflict with religious and civilizational confrontation (Todorov 2010), and insufficient attention to the heterogeneity of political culture within each major civilization (Sen 1999, 15–16; Voll and Esposito 1994). More broadly, many scholars have been disturbed by the blurring between purportedly dispassionate scholarly prediction and the conjuring up of civilizational animosities and discord (Herzog 1999; Tipson 1997; Bottici and Challand 2006). After the terrorist attacks of 9/11, however, Huntington received some more positive feedback (see e.g. Inglehart and Norris 2003; Betts 2010).

Twenty-five years on, what can usefully be added to this wealth of existing analysis? This chapter proposes a brief contemporary analysis of the empirical validity of the prediction – after all, Huntington's main goal was prognostic. Just as Huntington's article and book were, in essence, essays, so is this chapter. The focus is on the increasingly conflictual relations between Russia and the West as arguably the most important example of a purported 'civilizational' clash today. Can this clash be usefully analyzed in terms of discordant Orthodox and Western civilizations in line with Huntington? Theoretically, the chapter seeks to critically explore the Huntingtonian relationship between civilizations and regime types. In fact, for Huntington, civilizations are directly related to political systems, and this is important for understanding why they clash. However, the chapter argues that, rather than take a 'civilizational detour', it is more analytically fruitful to focus directly on how and why ideologically different political systems and regimes clash and how this can be circumvented. Doing so also avoids conflating regime interests and ideology from the more diverse interests and ideational viewpoints of citizens.

The Ukraine Crisis: A Civilizational 'Exhibit A'?

Huntington was primarily interested in explaining and predicting patterns of military tension and warfare. In this sense, the conflictual relations between Russia and the West can arguably be considered the most important example of a purportedly 'civilizational' clash today. The other main contender, the bloody Middle East conflagration is, in fact, pitting non-state armed groups, states, and coalitions of states from *within* the same Islamic civilization – aided by a variety of external powers – against each other: interestingly, Huntington did not even mention the Shia - Sunni divide in his 1993 article, although he did so, albeit rather briefly, in his book. Thus, the wars across the Arab world do not, as predicted, follow from a fault line conflict between Muslims and non-Muslims (Huntington 1996, 208), but constitute primarily an intra-Muslim conflagration.[1] A second possible contender, the (so far non-

---

[1]   The Mediterranean border between European Christendom and the post-Ottoman Islamic South (to employ a Huntingtonian vocabulary) is, in contrast very deadly. Over 12,200 deaths have been recorded during 2014–2016 in the Mediterranean

lethal) tensions around the South China Sea and the Koreas, are, again, 'intra-civilizational' border conflicts or, even, pitting two parts of the same nation (the two Koreas) against each other. There is of course a clear element of great power rivalry present, but to define these in civilizational terms does not seem to add anything to a classical Realist, power political understanding of the tensions (cf. Betts 2010).

It might seem futile to attempt to counter Huntington's broad-brush theoretical framework with one single case study, not least since Huntington himself stresses the generality of his theory and the fact that it is not meant to be exhaustive or apply to each case (Huntington 1996, 29–30 and 36–37). However, if his theory cannot explain a key defining feature of the present-day international security system, its utility is put in serious doubt. Moreover, though brief, the case study illustrates how important it is to move beyond facile and hastily drawn conclusions à la Huntington. Huntington may have created a sweeping and richly illustrated account, but breadth here becomes a main weakness: scratch the surface of an at first glance plausible set of illustrative cases, and another, more complex, pictures emerges.

The conflict over Ukraine is at the heart of the souring of relations between the West and Russia. It could at first glance be offered as the perfect civilizational 'Exhibit A'. Although Huntington is inconsistent in his argumentation[2], he explains that 'the most significant dividing line in Europe' is the eastern boundary of Western Christianity, inter alia cutting through Ukraine, thus 'separating the more Catholic Western Ukraine from Orthodox Eastern Ukraine' (Huntington 1993, 30). He seems almost prophetic when he writes:

(International Organization for Migration 2017). However, to analyze these deaths in terms of a religious or civilizational conflict between the two sides is hardly apposite: causes are to be found in the intra-Muslim conflagration mentioned above as well as economic and political conditions in parts of the Global South.

[2]   While he generally refers to Ukraine as a 'cleft country' encompassing large groups of people from two different civilizations (Huntington 1996, 137–138 and 165–167), he at the same time claims that:

"Common membership in a civilization reduces the probability of violence in situations where it might otherwise occur. In 1991 and 1992 many people were alarmed by the possibility of violent conflict between Russia and Ukraine over territory, particularly Crimea, the Black Sea Fleet, nuclear weapons and economic issues. If civilization is what counts, however, the likelihood of violence between Ukrainians and Russians should be low. They are two Slavic, primarily Orthodox peoples who have had close relationships with each other for centuries. As of early 1993, despite all the reasons for conflict, the leaders of the two countries were effectively negotiating and defusing the issues between the two countries (Huntington 1993, 38)."

> As one Russian general put it, 'Ukraine or rather Eastern Ukraine will come back in five, ten or fifteen years. Western Ukraine can go to hell'. Such a rump Uniate and Western-oriented Ukraine, however, would only be viable if it had strong and effective Western support. Such support is, in turn, likely to be forthcoming only if relations between the West and Russia deteriorated seriously and came to resemble those of the Cold War (Huntington 1996, 167–168).

In short, Crimea and Eastern Ukraine are located precisely on the civilizational fault line which Huntington predicted would be 'flash points for crisis and bloodshed', and what we are currently seeing is, indeed, a festering confrontation over these areas between Russia and the West.

However, this conclusion is too hasty. It is insufficient because it does not take into account how and why the conflict escalated in the first place. Russia was always testy on the issue of NATO and EU expansion, on grounds of power politics and spheres of influence rather than civilization (Haukkala 2015). However, it had for a number of years tolerated the European Union's Neighbourhood Policy (ENP), while trying to counter it with its own mix of soft and hard power projection (Averre 2009; Wiegand and Schulz 2015). For example, Russia had, however grudgingly, accepted EU *rapprochement* with countries in the Orthodox sphere, such as Serbia's status as an EU applicant state. Thus, Russian military intervention in Crimea and Eastern Ukraine because of a fear of Ukrainian 'Europeanization' through closer ties with the EU – which did not offer any meaningful prospect for membership – is a relative break with the recent past. Had this been a civilizational conflict, we should not logically have seen such a pronounced shift.

So what changed and led to escalation? Most authors agree that the fact that the successive successes of externally promoted so-called 'color revolutions' were creeping closer to Russian borders gradually changed perceptions in Moscow (Wilson 2010). Analysts see the extensive Russian anti-government protest movements in 2011 as a turning point: President Putin viewed them as a direct threat to the current Russian political system and hence to his own power, and, importantly, as orchestrated from the West (McFaul, 2014). The Russian regime came to fear what Western policy makers wished for, namely that 'consolidating a pro-Western, democratic Ukraine would indirectly encourage democratization in Russia' (Asmus 2008). In short, what we are seeing along the most conflictual of the so-called civilizational fault lines is not so much a civilizational conflict as a conflict over *political regimes* and a fear both of 'regime change' orchestrated from abroad and of loss of vital parts of the Russian traditional sphere of influence.

Civilizations, Political Systems, or Power Politics: What Do States Actually Clash Over?

But could not Huntington's theory accommodate for this? After all, according to Huntington's predictions, Western and non-Western states would clash mainly over two sets of issues, neither of which are civilizational *per se*. The first set of sources of interstate tension and conflict, Huntington predicted, would be economic competition, weapons proliferation, borders and the like – in short, classical issues of power politics. The second set was likely to be human rights, democracy, and institutions, which are all related to political systems or regime types (Huntington 1993, 40–41; Huntington 1996, Chapter eight). Although this is somewhat obfuscated by inconsistencies in his argumentation[3], Huntington's basic underlying assumption was that human rights are Western values and democracy is a Western system of rule. States from other civilizations have three alternatives. They can 'band-wagon', attempting 'to join the West and accept its values and institutions' (Huntington 1993, 41). Alternatively, they can pursue, at great cost, a course of isolation from all Western economic, cultural, political and military penetration and influence. The third and most commonly adopted solution is to 'balance' the West, by modernizing economically and militarily in line with Western models, while 'preserving indigenous values and institutions' (Huntington 1993, 41). Thus, for Huntington, civilizations are very intimately related to systems of rule: Western-led economic modernization may become virtually global, but democracy, the rule of law and human rights remain Western values and institutions. As a result, the vast majority of non-Western states that choose 'isolation' or 'balancing' can potentially clash with the West over such values.

However, the argument in this chapter is that the 'civilizational detour' made by Huntington – deriving differences in regime type from civilizational differences – is both redundant and misleading. It is more analytically fruitful to focus directly on how ideologically different systems of rule clash.

---

[3]   Intermittently, he sees democratization as a consequence of economic development and the social and political modernization that follows in its wake. Thus, for example, he writes – in line with classical Modernization Theory – that '[m]any Arab countries, in addition to the oil exporters, are reaching levels of economic and social development where autocratic forms of government become inappropriate and efforts to introduce democracy become stronger. Some openings in Arab political systems have already occurred...' (Huntington 1993, 32) and in another instance he argues that '[i]n the former Soviet Union, communists can become democrats, the rich can become poor and the poor rich, but Russians cannot become Estonians and Azeris cannot become Armenians' (Huntington 1993, 27). Both of course imply that democratic values can well go beyond the Western sphere. There is thus, throughout Huntington's account, a tension between modernization theory and civilizational explanations for how and why democracy can arise.

The 'civilizational detour' is redundant, as fears over regime stability and survival combined with Realist spheres of influence explanations are sufficient to explain the main current purported 'civilizational' clash pitting Russia against the West as discussed above (statistical analysis of conflict patterns since the end of the Cold War have reached similar conclusions regarding the paramount importance of Realist (and to a lesser extent Liberal) explanations for warfare) (see e.g. Russett et al 2000; Henderson and Tucker 2001). Adding the contradiction between Orthodoxy and Western Christendom into the explanatory equation does not give it more power. For someone like Huntington, who is interested in parsimony and explanatory power, this is an important consideration (Huntington 1996, 29–30).

The 'civilizational detour' is also misleading. It is pointing to civilizational incompatibilities as the ultimate causes of conflict, when conflict over alternative political systems is clearly a more pertinent factor in explaining today's clash between Russia and the West. Increasingly, the West and Russia are – just as during the Cold War – pitching two alternative political systems against each other: one more strongly focused on liberal democracy, individualism, and the rule of law, the other with an emphasis on nationalism, order, and 'traditional' values. This is also manifest in the conduct of foreign policy. Thus, apart from pursuing a classical policy of economic, political, and military sticks and carrots in its near abroad, the Russian leadership is also promoting 'its' values in neighboring states, helping to maintain in power those leaders with a similar ideological outlook (Finkel and Brudny 2012). The Russian government has also supported political groupings and parties in the West – including most famously the National Front in France and the Republican candidate (now President) Donald Trump in the US – that it sees as ideologically close. In so doing, the Russian government is not promoting Christian Orthodoxy or any particularly 'Russian' values, but rather classical authoritarian values such as nationalism, conservatism and patriarchy. It is doing so in response to Western democracy promotion, a constant, if not consistently applied, feature of US and European foreign policy over several decades (Diamond 2008; Robinson 1996; Schumacher *et al* 2017). Indeed, we might be witnessing a return to Cold War patterns of competitive value promotion globally.[4]

---

[4]   During the Cold War, the US, through *inter alia* Radio Free Europe and support for the Polish trade union Solidarity and other opposition groups, was trying to undermine the Soviet bloc. The USSR reciprocated through its support for European communist parties and covert attempts at trying to influence public opinion in Western states. Today, we see a return to a similar pattern of policies and activities: Russia, now a nationalistic, authoritarian and anti-liberal power, supports like-minded parties and movements in the West and beyond, tries to use new and old media to influence public opinion, etc.; the US pursues a similar policy through specific media outlets, foreign aid, and support for non-governmental organizations. After the end of the Cold War, US

The 'civilizational detour' is also misleading in that it conflates the interests of the rulers and those of the ruled. Just as liberal democracy, individualism, and the rule of law are not universally accepted in the West – and are indeed threatened by several Western political actors and groups, including those supported by the regime of Vladimir Putin – so are nationalism, conservatism, and patriarchy not supported across the board in non-Western societies. Moreover, popular support for particular sets of political values undergoes important shifts over time within the same purported civilization. As noted by Russett *et al*, 'the political cultures of Germany and Japan changed radically after 1945 from their prewar fascism, in both cases becoming democratic and substantially anti-militarist. Yet both Germany and Japan remain deeply rooted in their distinctive civilizations' (Russett et al 2000, 587).

Does this mean that Huntington's policy prescriptions regarding the international promotion of democracy, human rights and the rule of law were wrong? In his book, Huntington roundly criticized 'crusading democrats' (Huntington 1996, 65), coolly noting that, historically, '[t]he West won the world not by the superiority of its ideas or values or religion… but rather by its superiority in applying organized violence. Westerners often forget this fact; non-Westerners never do' (Huntington 1996, 51). For him, 'The central problem in the relations between the West and the rest is… the discordance between the West's – particularly America's – efforts to promote a universal Western culture and its declining ability to do so' (Huntington 1996, 183). The only way for the West to shape non-Western societies in its mold would be through 'the expansion, deployment, and impact of Western power. Imperialism is the necessary logical consequence of universalism' (Huntington 1996, 310). Moreover, Western states will have other interests which will regularly trump their democratic and human rights principles, leading to hypocrisy and double standards (Huntington 1996, 184). The wiser alternative, Huntington argued, was to accept that '[t]he security of the world requires acceptance of global multiculturality' (Huntington 1996, 318).[5]

Western governments have clearly not followed Huntington's advice in this respect. Democracy promotion policies have remained a constant in their foreign policy and foreign aid toolboxes. Results have been mixed at best, with analysts regularly decrying inconsistencies and double standards, much

---

activities have been complemented by EU and European governmental democracy assistance programs (largely absent during the Cold War). The Western, as well as non-Western, response to international value promotion on the home turf has been mixed: some states have remained open to external value promotion activities within its borders; others have reacted by trying to restrict it.

[5]   Again, Huntington is not entirely consistent, at one point noting that the US 'must forge alliances with similar cultures and spread its values wherever possible' (Huntington 1993).

as Huntington noted. In the academic literature, there has been considerable debate regarding the type of democracy promoted by Western states, the cautious and non-confrontational nature of democracy promotion in some recipient countries, the declining effectiveness of various democracy promotion strategies over time, the political and strategic context of democracy promotion, its potentially adverse effects on political developments in autocratic states, etc. More rarely have academics debated the future of the agenda as a whole.

The answer to the question 'should democracy be promoted in autocratic states?' might not have to be as categorical as both Huntington and Western governments would have it (Huntington wrote that [d]eep imperatives within American culture… impel the United States to be at least a nanny if not a bully in international affairs' (Huntington 1996, 226–227)). It might be better to leave to civil society the world over the task of promoting democracy, human rights, and the rule of law, thereby forging more genuine and less inconsistent agendas and partnerships across national, religious, and ideological boundaries.

Conclusions

Huntington predicted that civilizational differences – largely based on religious divides – would lead the 'West and the rest' to clash. His 'clash of civilizations' has become something of a political myth (Bottici and Challand 2006) while sparking considerable academic controversy. This chapter argues that an in-depth analysis of Huntington's argumentation reveals the importance he accords to human rights and democracy as the basic cause of division between the 'West and the rest'. In fact, his underlying assumption is that human rights and democracy are Western values. Thus, in fact, for Huntington, civilizations are directly related to political systems, and this is important for understanding why they clash.

The argument proposed here is that it is more analytically fruitful to focus directly on how ideologically different political systems clash. This becomes particularly clear in the case of the increasingly conflictual relations between Russia and the West, which is the most important example of a purported 'civilizational' clash today. With Ukraine at center stage, this conflict at first glance seems to confirm Huntington's thesis to the letter, as he identifies Catholic Western Ukraine - Orthodox Eastern Ukraine as a civilizational 'flash point'. However, such an analysis does not take into account how and why the conflict occurred: because of increasing Russian fear of externally promoted so-called 'color revolutions', in particular after the extensive anti-government protest movements inside Russia itself in 2011. President Putin viewed these as a direct threat to the current Russian political system, and as orchestrated from the West.

Thus, what we are seeing along the most conflictual of the so-called civilizational fault lines is not so much a civilizational conflict as a conflict over alternative political systems. It pits liberal democracy, individualism and the rule of law against authoritarianism, nationalism, order and 'traditional' values. At the same time, it is becoming increasingly clear that these fault lines are also found within, rather than between, so-called civilizations. Power politics and ideology, in contrast with Huntington's predictions, are alive and well. In this context, democracy promotion agendas of Western states have become more central to power politics and their future should arguably be more widely debated.

References

Ajami, Fouad. 1993. "The Summoning." *Foreign Affairs* 72(4): 2–9.

Asmus, Ronald D. 2008. "Europe's Eastern Promise: Rethinking NATO and EU Enlargement." *Foreign Affairs* 87(1): 95–106.

Averre, Derek. 2009. "Competing Rationalities: Russia, the EU and the 'Shared Neighbourhood.'" *Europe-Asia Studies* 61(10): 1689–1713.

Betts, Richard K. 2010. "Conflict or Cooperation? Three Visions Revisited." *Foreign Affairs* 89(6): 186–194.

Bottici, Chiara and Benoît Challand. 2006. "Rethinking Political Myth: The Clash of Civilizations as a Self-Fulfilling Prophecy." *European Journal of Social Theory* 9(3): 315–336.

Diamond, Larry. 2008. *The Spirit of Democracy: The Struggle to Build Free Societies Throughout the World*. New York: St. Martin's Griffin.

Finkel, Evgeny and Yitzhak M. Brudny. 2012. "No More Colour! Authoritarian Regimes and Colour Revolutions in Eurasia." *Democratization* 19(1): 1–14.

Fox, Jonathan. 2001. "Clash of Civilizations or Clash of Religions: Which is a More Important Determinant of Ethnic Conflict?." *Ethnicities* 1(3): 295–320.

Haukkala, Hiski. 2015. "From Cooperative to Contested Europe? The Conflict in Ukraine as a Culmination of a Long-Term Crisis in EU –Russia Relations." *Journal of Contemporary European Studies* 23(1): 25–40.

Henderson, Errol A. and Richard Tucker. 2001. "Clear and Present Strangers: The Clash of Civilizations and International Conflict." *International Studies Quarterly*, 45(2):317–338.

Huntington, Samuel P. 1996. *The Clash of Civilizations and the Remaking of World Order.* London: Touchstone Books.

Huntington, Samuel P. 1993. "The Clash of Civilizations?" *Foreign Affairs* 72(3): 22–49.

Inglehart, Ronald, and Pippa Norris. 2003. "The True Clash of Civilizations." *Foreign Policy* (March/April): 63–70.

International Organization for Migration. 2017. "Missing Migrants: Tracking Deaths Along Migratory Routes." *International Organization for Migration.* https://missingmigrants.iom.int/ Accessed 19 October 2017.

Mahbubani, Kishore. 1993. "The Dangers of Decadence." *Foreign Affairs* 72(4): 10.

McFaul, Michael. 2014. "Moscow's Choice." *Foreign Affairs*, 93(6): 167–171.

Robinson, William I. 1996. *Promoting Polyarchy: Globalization, US Intervention, and Hegemony.* Cambridge: Cambridge University Press.

Russett, Bruce M., John R. O'Neal and Michaelene Cox. 2000. "Clash of Civilizations, or Realism and Liberalism Déjà Vu? Some Evidence." *Journal of Peace Research* 37(5): 583–608.

Sen, Amartya. 1999. "Democracy as a Universal Value." *Journal of Democracy* 10(3): 3–17.

Schumacher, Tobias, Andreas Marchetti and Thomas Demmelhuber, eds. 2018. *The Routledge Handbook on the European Neighbourhood Policy.* Oxford: Routledge.

Tipson, Frederick S. 1997. "Culture Clash-ification: A Verse to Huntington's Curse." *Foreign Affairs* 76(2): 166–169.

Todorov, Tzvetan. 2010. *The Fear of Barbarians: Beyond the Clash of Civilizations.* Chicago: University of Chicago Press.

Voll, John O. and John L. Esposito. 1994. "Islam's Democratic Essence." *Middle East Quarterly* 1(3).

Wiegand Gunnar and Evelina Schulz. 2015. "The EU and Its Eastern Partnership: Political Association and Economic Integration in a Rough Neighbourhood," In *Trade Policy between Law, Diplomacy and Scholarship. European Yearbook of International Economic Law*, edited by Herrmann C., Simma B. and Rudolf Streinz. Springer.

Wilson, Jeanne L. 2010. "The Legacy of the Color Revolutions for Russian Politics and Foreign Policy." *Problems of Post-Communism* 57(2): 21–3.

9

Where Does Russia End and the West Start?

ANNA TIIDO

If you stand on the banks of the river Narva in North-Eastern Europe, you can see two medieval castles facing each other on both sides of the river. These castles are a powerful symbol of the border between Russia and Estonia, a border that, in our times, also separates the European Union and NATO from Russia. The question is: Is it also the fault line between two distinctive civilizations (Western and Orthodox)? According to Huntington in his 1993 article 'The Clash of Civilizations?', the great division among humankind in the new phase will be cultural, the 'clash of civilizations' will dominate global politics. The fault lines between civilizations will be the battle lines of the future. Has this new phase arrived? This article will argue that the Estonia/ Russia border is indeed a fault line between the Western and Russian civilizations, and it leads to simmering conflict. This conflict also exists inside the Estonian society, as a large minority of Russian speakers reside in Estonia.

To the East of Narva, the vast plains stretching through the Ural Mountains to the coasts of the Pacific Ocean form the territory of the Russian state. Samuel Huntington cites Carroll Quigley in distinguishing the Orthodox (Russian) civilization as emerging from the Classical (Mediterranean) one, but taking on a separate path later (Huntington 1996, 49). Huntington considers Russia creating a bloc with an Orthodox heartland. At the same time, according to Huntington, Russia is a torn country with its identity in permanent crisis (Huntington 1996, 164). It is important to note here that the Russian identity has always been defined in opposition to the 'significant other', and this other has always been the West. The West was either positive or negative, but it is always present in the visions of national identity and national interest (Tsygankov 2006, 17).

There were several attempts to modernize Russia during the course of history. One famous attempt of modernization and Europeanization was undertaken by Peter the Great in the eighteenth century. Later on, in the nineteenth century, the debate between Slavophiles and Westerners dominated the intellectual debate in Russia. Relevant for our times is the experiment with democracy of the 1990s, when the authorities of Russia undertook radical reforms at home, and took a pro-Western course in foreign policy. The opinion leaders and policymakers of Russia could be divided according to their foreign policy attitudes into Westernizers, Statists and Civilizationists. Westernizers placed the emphasis on Russia's similarities with the West, the importance of liberal values such as human rights, democracy and free market. Statists, in contrast, chose the values of stability, power and sovereignty over freedom and democracy. The statist main purpose though was pragmatic, defending the Russian national interest by geopolitical means. Civilizationists, on the other hand, saw Russian values as distinct from the West, and they wanted to spread these values around the world. Their response to the issues of the security of Russia was more aggressive than the Statists'. Statists basically think of defending the status quo and play the geopolitical game, they are not against negotiations with others. For Civilizationists, the Russian civilization is seen as superior, and this approach is connected to the 'Third Rome' dictum, and the 'gathering of Russian lands' (Tsygankov 2006, 7).

The discourse of Civilizationism has started to dominate official Russian policy since the authority of Vladimir Putin was established. The ideas of Civilizationists and Eurasianists started penetrating official statements in the 2000s, especially after the attempt at rapprochement with the West, and further drifted apart after. The frequency of the terms 'morality' and 'spiritual' in Putin's speeches increased, especially since his return to the Presidency in 2012. In his article of 2012, 'Russia, the National Question', Putin says that 'the goals of our foreign policy are strategic rather than short-term. They reflect Russia's unique role in international affairs, in history and in the development of civilization' (Putin 2012). What came to be called Putin's conservative agenda, includes such values as heterosexual family, an emphasis on having children as a basis for individual life but also for the country's demographic health; the fight against alcoholism; and respect for the elderly and for hierarchy (Laurelle 2015). In the nineteenth century, the issue of the unique Russian civilization was typically raised by conservative philosophers, especially Nikolay Danilevsky and Konstantin Leontiev. In the 1990s and later, Russian philosopher and ideologist Alexander Dugin has claimed consistently that Russia is a civilization rather than a nation. Dugin started as a figure separate from the authorities, but his ideas slowly moved into the mainstream, and became very important to the establishment. Already in his book *The Foundations of the Geopolitics* in 1997 he writes that:

The Russian people, as different from many other peoples has been formed as a carrier of unique civilization, which has all the distinct features of original and full planetary-historic phenomenon. The Russian people is the constant, which served as an axis for creation of not one, but many states: from the mosaic of the dukedoms of Eastern Slavs, Moscovite Rus, the Empire of Peter the Great and the Soviet bloc. (…) The Russian people did not just provide for the ethnic base for all of these state formations, but it expressed a special civilizational idea, unlike any other. It is not the state that formed the nation. The other way around, the Russian people, the Russian nation has been experimenting in history with different types of state systems, expressing in a different way (depending on circumstances) the specificity of its unique mission. The Russian people certainly belong to the messianic peoples. As any messianic people, it has universal all-human meaning, which competes not just with other national ideas, but other forms of civilizational universalism (Dugin 1997, 191).

As we can see, the ideas of Dugin are Civilizationist, he sees the Russian civilization as universal. The blurriness of Russianness, and Russia being not only a state, but also a civilization is connected also to the fact that Russians do not live only on the territory of the Russian state. Russians outside Russia are an important resource and inspiration for the policies of Russia. The main policies concerning Russians outside Russia are the policy of compatriots, and the more general framework policy of the 'Russian World'. Actually, one can see the evolution from the more defined and, one could argue, bureaucratic policy of compatriots towards much more blurred and definitely more emotional trend of claiming the 'Russian World'. We can see the trend from the policy with concrete measures, such as repatriation, towards an overwhelming 'Russianness'. At the extreme end of this spectrum one can place the symbolic saying of Putin that Russia has no borders at all, which later was interpreted as a joke (RT 2016). The important document, where the legal concept of compatriots comes from, is the 'The Federal Law on the State Policy of the Russian Federation in Relation to Compatriots Abroad' of 1999. This law actually does not define precisely who a 'compatriot' is. Legally speaking, according to the law, a compatriot is any citizen of Tsarist Russia, Soviet Russia or the Soviet Union. The compatriots are also descendants of other states' citizens who do not belong to the 'titular' nation ('titular' meaning the ethnic nations of the former Soviet Union's non-Russian republics – the word itself means the ethnic nation present in the name of the state, e.g., France - French, Estonia - Estonian) and are presumably Russian-speaking. In the same way, anyone who feels linked to Russia considers himself or herself a compatriot – in such a case, this category is no longer a legal one, but an ethno-psychological one. Not just the law, but Russian discourse in general, has ambiguous definitions of compatriots. In 2001, after the law was in force, Vladimir Putin said that

> ... a compatriot is not a purely legal category. And even further – it is not a question of status or any advantages. This is, first and foremost, the question of personal choice. The question of self-determination. I would even say more precisely – of spiritual choice. This way is not always easy (Putin 2001).

Similar statements appeared in the media at the time from other officials. In 2001, Vladimir Putin signed the new document 'The concept of supporting by the Russian Federation of the compatriots abroad at the present stage', in which the notion of a 'compatriot' is even blurrier. 'Persons permanently living outside of Russian Federation, but connected to Russia by historic, ethnic, cultural, language and spiritual links, who strive to preserve their Russian originality (*самобытность*) and willing to keep contacts and cooperate with Russia' (Самородний 2014, 71).

We can see the tendency from trying to embrace compatriots into the legal framework of the Russian Federation towards leaving this concept quite blurred. The manifestation of the Russianness is becoming a more emotional concept with the emergence of the so-called 'Russian World'. The term 'Russian World' was used in medieval accounts to define ancient Rus. It can be traced to the 11th century in the writings of Russian Grand Prince of Kiev Iziaslav Iaroslavich, who spoke of a 'Kherson and Russian World' in a letter addressed to the Roman Pope Clement (Laruelle 2012). The term seems to have been taken from his account in the nineteenth century by Count Sergey Uvarov (1786–1855), president of the Imperial Academy of Sciences and minister of education, famous for having crafted the tripartite emblem of the reign of Czar Nicholas I: 'Autocracy, Orthodoxy, Nationality'. However, the term was not commonly used, and preference was given to other concepts. The founding father of Slavophilism, Aleksei Khomyakov (1804–1860), spoke of the 'Russian spirit' (*русский дух*), the Silver Age philosophers Vladimir Soloviev and Nikolay Berdiaev of the 'Russian idea' (*русская идея*), and it is as common in Russia as in the West to encounter the idea of the 'Russian soul' (*русская душа*) when assuming that Russia is eternally miscomprehended.

The current, post-Soviet term of the 'Russian World' emerged in the end of the 1990s. In their 1999 article, Petr Shchedrovitsky and Efim Ostrovsky elaborated on their definition of the Russian World. According to them:

Over the course of the twentieth century, following tectonic historical shifts, world wars and revolutions, a Russian World was created on Earth – a network of small and large communities, thinking and speaking in Russian. It is not a secret that the territory of the Russian Federation contains only half of this Russian World. The state formation created on the territory of the Russian Federation at the turn of the 1990s did not turn out to be an adequate means for incorporating Russian society into the global historical process. (...) This process of social degradation (the collapse of the Soviet Union) has been compensated by the formation, over the course of the twentieth century, of a sizeable Russian diaspora in the world (Островский 1999).

In conclusion, the article highlights the innovative character of the Russian World as a sign of a new, globalized Russia: 'A Russian World in a Peaceful World (*русский мир в мире миров*), attracting Russians from all over the world to participate in a new global meta-project' (Laruelle 2015). The Russian World is characterized by a dual aspect: it is a brand for establishing Russia's voice in the chorus of nations, but it is also a vessel for a more philosophical or religious messianism, with the notion that Russia's message to the world has a universal value of salvation (Laruelle 2015). It is also important to note that in Russian, the term «мир» has not only one meaning ('world'), but also the meaning of community, village community first of all, of 'everybody' in a sense. It also has a third meaning – peace. The role of the Orthodox Church in Russia cannot be underestimated. It can be well explained by Huntington's claim of the revival of religion in the world of the 'clash of civilizations'. He specifically mentions Russia, where Orthodoxy had gone through a major resurgence (Huntington 1996, 96).

It can be easily claimed that the recent revival of civilizational rhetoric is purely instrumental, and done with geopolitical purposes in mind. I claim that the thesis of Huntington is more relevant to explain the moves of Russian authorities. It is a conflict of different cultures and even emotions that drives Russia away from the West and into elaborating its own peculiar civilization.

We could see now into the formation of attitudes in Russia, in what concerns the Russians abroad. What about the Western bank of Narva? The region of the Baltics has been populated for a long time, more than 6000 years since the end of the Stone Age. People known as Estonians or Aesti have been living here for around 1500 years (Raun 2001, 3). The origins of Finno-Ugric tribes are obscure. The first major theory by the Finnish scholar M.A. Castren in the nineteenth century postulated that a common homeland for the Uralic and Altaic peoples was in the Altaic mountains of South-Eastern Siberia (Raun 2001, 6). Later, the ideas which denied the common origin of all these peoples emerged. By the present day, these peoples preserved their languages, which are not part of the Indo-European group. Later on, in the 13th century, these pagan tribes fought the Livonian Order and were finally occupied by them. It has been the beginning of the settlement of the German-speaking landed gentry on these territories. The first encounters with the Slavs took place early on, especially well-known is the conquest of the settlement of Tarbatu (present day Tartu) by the Prince Yaroslav in 1030 (Miljan 2015, XXV).

The Livonian Order had some designs on the Slav lands to the East, and there were several armed conflicts. After many devastating wars, and especially the Nordic Seven Years War (1563–1570), Estonia, at the time known as Livonia, fell under Swedish rule. This period is still sometimes referred to colloquially as 'good old Swedish time' (Kõiv 2000). What later came to be called the 'Northern War' broke out in the region in 1707. It was connected to the tsar of Russia, Peter the Great's policies of expanding to the West, and needing the 'window to Europe', as St. Petersburg was referred to (Ponsard 2007, 11). After 1721, Estonian territory became part of the Russian Empire and it remained this way until 1918.

It is important to remember that by this time, Estonians were Protestants, and this led to the high level of literacy in their mother tongue, as everybody had to listen to the sermons in their native language and also know how to read the Catechesis. Thus, Estonian language education was spreading, and with time, the number of educated Estonians reached critical mass, which served as a basis for reconstruction of historic memory and emergence of independent thinking (Laidre 2001, 85). It can also be claimed that according to the famous thesis of Max Weber, Protestantism led to the high morals and work ethics among the population. Max Weber notes that the German word for profession is *Beruf* or 'calling', the same is true about the Estonian language – *elukutse* is 'calling' or, more precisely, 'life calling'. Thus, Protestantism claimed that you can achieve unity with God through your work, through your profession. Huntington also claims that there is a correlation between democracy and Protestantism, with many and first Protestant states becoming democracies (Huntington 1991, 37). Protestantism has great influence on the values of Estonians still, and these values sometimes clash with the Orthodox ideas of ethnic Russians.

With the reign of Peter the Great, not much changed in the constitution of society: German aristocracy kept their privileges, the German language was used in administration, and Peter the Great actually called the new provinces his 'German provinces' (Faure and Mensing 2012, 119). Few Russian aristocrats owned the land in these territories. This arrangement was called 'Baltic special order' in the Russian Empire. It must be noted that the Russian Empire did not see the necessity of forceful assimilation of the newly acquired lands and was rather tolerant towards different confessions. Its way of ruling was by using local aristocracy, and the German barons were also serving the Empire in the capital.

The Estonian people remained *maarahvas* or 'countryside folks' not having many opportunities for social mobility and being mainly peasants. For these people, both German aristocracy and Russians masters were 'others', and this is how the Estonian identity was formed. In the nineteenth century, the national awakening was taking place among Estonians echoing the overall European process of nationalist ideas. The Estonian model has its roots in the ideas of Johann Gottfried von Herder. For Herder, nationalism was more a cultural phenomenon than a political one (Schmidt 1956). As there was no state of Estonians, the emphasis on ethnicity mattered more. Thus, it has deep roots, which help us understand modern processes better. It was also during this time when under the rule of the Russian tsar Alexander the Third, the policy of 'russification' started.

By 1918, the opportunity presented itself, after the devastating First World War, Bolshevist Revolution, and the Brest-Litovsk settlement. The Estonian Republic was proclaimed, followed by the War of Independence against Soviet Russia and *Landeswehr*, the forces of Baltic German aristocracy. The Estonian Republic existed until the 1940 occupation by the Soviet Union, which happened as a direct result of the Molotov-Ribbentrop Pact of 1939, and its secret protocol dividing this part of Europe into spheres of influence. The German occupation followed in 1941, and then Soviet occupation again in 1944, which lasted until 1991. Soviet authorities applied cruel policies of repression against the Estonian population including mass arrests and deportations to Siberia. After the Second World War, massive migration was conducted to the territory of Estonia, and a 1989 Soviet census established that about 30% of the population of the Estonian Soviet Socialist Republic were non-Estonians. They mainly came to work for the industries, and mostly they did not master the Estonian language (around 15% of newcomers spoke Estonian) (Rudensky 1994, 63). Another wave of 'russification' followed, when Russian became the language of communication in many spheres. As Perestroika started in the 1980s, there were the language issues, which were high on the agenda in Estonia, as the situation with the Estonian language was the most important problem next to the demand for autonomy (Rannut 2004, 5). The language law was adopted by the Supreme Soviet of Estonian SSR in 1989. The process of transformation is closely connected to the Singing revolution of civic disaccord with the Soviet rule starting around 1987, protests against new projects of Soviet rule, such as the phosphorite excavation. There was an extraordinary show of solidarity in 1989 of the Baltic republics known as the Baltic chain, when about two million people from Tallinn to Vilnius joined hands to remind the world of the Molotov-Ribbentrop pact. Notwithstanding attempts at russification, the Estonian identity was preserved as strong all through the years of all the occupations and mistreatment.

Estonian identity developed in close connection with Western civilization, and naturally, after the declaration of independence in 1991, the main goal of the government was its reintegration with the West. The foreign policy of Estonia was flowing naturally from its source – the need to re-establish a nation-state based on the national identity of the majority ethnic group. The first goal was to ensure that the independence was for real, and thus, the Russian troops withdrawal was a must (Kauppila 1994). It took years of painful negotiations until 1994 when the last Russian soldier left Estonian soil. The border negotiations were conducted simultaneously, and this story is not yet finished, as the Russian Duma has not ratified the border agreements at the time of writing of this article.

The second important objective of foreign policy was integration with the European Union and NATO institutions. The difficult negotiations led to the integration into these organizations in 2004. During these negotiations, Estonia had to get rid of its Soviet legacy and prove that it truly belonged to the West. The new institutions were formed and sustained. Especially important was the establishment of the rule of law according to Western standards. To this day, the judicial system functions properly. Estonia continues to rank high among countries according to the index of perception of corruption, placed on the 22nd position in 2016 (Transparency International 2017). Estonian Minister of Foreign Affairs, Toomas Hendrik Ilves said in 1998,

> Estonia opted for a crash course in reforms and, as a result, enormous progress has been made since 1991: national and municipal elections have been completely free and open, the Estonian press is free and independent and there are thriving non-governmental organizations in every sphere of public life (Ilves 1998).

The development of capitalism led to a thriving economy. By now, more than 71% of the Estonian GDP is derived from the service sectors, industrial sectors yield 25% and primary branches (including agriculture) approximately four percent of the overall output (Invest in Estonia, n.d.)

Estonia was left with the legacy of about 27% of non-Estonians residing on the Estonian territory. The first reaction of Estonians was to ignore and neglect this issue – maybe the Russians would all move back 'home'? There were plans of repatriation and strict citizenship and language polices were adopted. The main principle of the policies was that of restitution – meaning that the Estonian Republic was the legal descendant of the pre-war Republic, and not a new state. This is a crucial principle in order to understand everything else going on in the society. Citizenship was granted to everybody whose ancestors were residing in the pre-war republic, notwithstanding their ethnicity. All the people who came later had to pass the process of naturalization – meaning pass an Estonian language exam and demonstrate knowledge of the Constitution and citizenship legislation. It led to the situation where about one third of the minority population have no citizenship and are considered aliens. At the same time, it also enabled pro-Western policies, as there was no opposition in the Parliament to the course of reintegration with the West.

By mid-1990s, Estonians realized that the Russians were a part of society, and they would not be leaving. It had been the start of the so-called integration policy. This is the policy of the inclusion into the society, though it first primarily concentrated on the need for non-Estonians to improve their command of the Estonian language. The general idea of the integration policy is to replace the attitude of 'non-Estonians as a problem' with the attitude 'non-Estonians as development potential'. The direction towards integration took place under the influence of three factors: the results of the academic research, the changing of political values, and the pressure from international organizations (Kallas, Mihkelsoo and Plaan 2012, 9).

In order to map the tendencies in integration, the Integration Monitorings are undertaken every now and then, the most recent results are of 2015 and 2017. The Monitoring of 2017 showed that command of the Estonian language among non-Estonians is improving, and the majority of the population supports starting with Estonian language instruction in kindergarten. The results show though that the majority of both Estonians and non-Estonians communicate in their own language space (Kaldur et al. 2017, 99). The results of various research also shows that it is not only the command of the Estonian language that divides the society, but the attitudes towards many issues are different for the two communities. In nowadays society, the difference of values is manifested in many ways, such as family patterns, attitudes towards LGBTI, the role of religion in life, state policies – in general, one can claim that Russians are more conservative in relation to these issues.

The attitudes towards LGBTI were thoroughly researched in 2014, and the data showed clear differences according to the major communication language of the respondents. Forty-nine percent of the Estonian-language respondents accepted homosexuality, with this number being just 21% for the Russian-speakers. Forty-four percent of Estonians and 73% of Russian-speakers did not accept homosexuality (Turu-uuringute AS 2017). Attitudes towards religion were researched in 2015 and the results showed that 19% of Estonians and 25% of non-Estonians belong to a congregation with 46% of Estonians and 80% of non-Estonians having been baptized. Forty percent of the overall population considers itself Orthodox, and 36% considers itself Lutheran (Saarpoll OÜ 2015). The main clash in opinions, though, is going along the lines of the attitudes towards Russia and its policies, with the majority of Estonians seeing its assertive behavior as a threat, and the Russians seeing the need for better relations with the Russian state. Thus, 79% of Estonians consider NATO membership to be a security guarantee, while only 28% of Russian-speakers do. At the same time, 67% of Russian-speakers consider cooperation and good relations with Russia a security guarantee, and this number is only 13% for Estonians (Kivirähk 2015, 20).

The recent study of the Estonian society 'Estonian society in the accelerating times. The results of the survey "Me. World. Media." 2002–2014' analyzed, among other things, the ethnic identities of Estonia's residents. One of the conclusions is that ethnic belonging is becoming dominant in comparison with other political identities – it is becoming the central identity a person applies to their self. Ethnic identity, both for majority and minority groups, is based not on political, but on cultural-religious symbols, values and practices, as one's ethnic belonging is perceived as the opposite of territorial or political solidarity. The Estonian Russian population has developed a strong identity based on ethno-cultural and religious roots expressing ethnic opposition and spiritual solidarity. It has happened, according to the research results, as a reaction to societal developments which are considered negative by the minority (Vihalemm et al. 2017, 134).

Conclusion

Now we are coming towards the interaction between these two states and societies, which we see are quite diverse. We could see the differences in culture and attitudes that support Huntington's thesis of an Orthodox civilization as distinct from the West. Estonia belongs to the West with its history, culture and values. Russian Orthodox civilization influences the attitudes of Russians in Estonia a great deal. As Huntington also puts it, Russia has a 'kin-state syndrome' towards Russians outside Russia (Huntington 1996, 272). We can see that the present Russian state's orientation on civilizational discourse leads to the situation that many Russians abroad can identify themselves with Russia without taking any everyday practical decisions, such as repatriation. The Russians in Estonia live their everyday life in the European Union. At the same time, they preserve their emotional link to Russia. This phenomenon could be described as transnationalism, as the transnational audience preserves the double reference framework, as they constantly compare their situation to that of their kin-state (Vihalemm et al. 2017, 598). In a way, Russians outside Russia become 'more Catholic than the Pope', because they see the reality of their countries of residence and compare it with the virtual reality created by the Russian state media. We could see that the 'clash of civilizations' is happening both between the states of Estonia and Russia, and at the same time in the minds of the Estonian population, as the Russian minority is influenced by the Orthodox civilization.

References

Дугин, Александр. 1997. Основы геополитики. Геополитическое будущее России.[The Foundations of Geopolitics. Geopolitical Future of Russia.] Арктогея, Москва [in Russian].

Самородний, Олег. 2014. *Соотечественники Кремля*. *[The Compatriots of Kremlin]*. Kärdla [in Russian].

Faure, Gunter and Teresa M. Mensing. 2012. *The Estonians; The Long Road to Independence.* Gunter Faure and Teresa M. Mensing.

Huntington, Samuel P. 1991. *The Third Wave: Democratization in the Late Twentieth Century*. University of Oklahoma Press: Norman and London.

Huntington, Samuel P. 1996. *The Clash of Civilizations and the Remaking of World Order.* Simon and Schuster. New York.

Ilves, Toomas Hendrik. 1998. "Estonia's Return to Europe." Public lecture. http://vm.ee/en/news/estonias-return-europe Accessed 30 July 2017.

Invest in Estonia. n.d. "Economy Overview." https://investinestonia.com/business-in-estonia/estonian-economy/ Accessed 07 November 2017.

Kaldur, Kristjan, Raivo Vetik, Kaura Kirss, Kats Kivistik, Külliki Seppel, Kristina

Kallas, Märt Masso and Kristi Anniste. 2017. *Eesti ühiskonna integratsiooni monitooring [The Integration Monitoring of Estonian Society].* Balti uuringute Instituut [in Estonian].

Kallas, Kristina, Ingi Mihkelsooand Kaarin Plaan. 2012. "Lõimuv Eesti 2000-2011. Integratsiooni monitooringute analüüs." [Integrating Estonia 2000–2011. The Analysis of the Integration Monitorings]. Institute of Baltic Studies [in Estonian].

Kauppila, Laura Eleonora. 1999. *The Baltic Puzzle: Russia's Policy towards Estonia and Lativa 1992–1997.* University of Helsinki.

Kivirähk, Juhan. 2015. *Avalik arvamus ja riigikaitse. [Public opinion and National defence].* Tellija: Kaitseministeerium. Turu-uuringute AS [in Estonian]. http://www.kaitseministeerium.ee/sites/default/files/elfinder/article_files/avalik_arvamus_ja_riigikaitse_marts_2015.pdf. Accessed 03 March 2016.

Kõiv, Lea. 2000. "The Great Northern War. End of Swedish Rule in Estonia." http://www.estonica.org/en/History/1558-1710_Estonia_under_Swedish_rule/The_Great_Northern_War_End_of_Swedish_rule_in_Estonia/ Accessed 07 November 2017.

Laidre, Margus. 2001. "Reformatsioonist rahvusliku ärkamiseni. 1520–1850." [From Reformation to the National Awakening. 1520–1850]. In *Eesti identiteet ja iseseisvus [Estonian Identity and Independence].* Avita [In Estonian].

Laruelle, Marlene. 2015. "The 'Russian World': Russia's Soft Power and Geopolitical Imagination." *Center on Global Interests*.

Turu-uuringute AS. 2017. "Avaliku arvamuse uuring LGBT teemadel." The Survey of Public Opinion on LGBT Topic [in Estonian]. https://humanrights.ee/app/uploads/2017/05/Avaliku-arvamuse-uuring-LGBT-teemadel-2017-4.pdf. Accessed 28 August 2017.

Miljan, Toivo. 2015. *Historical Dictionary of Estonia.* Rowman and Littlefield.

Островский Е., Щедровицкий П. 1999. Россия: страна, которой не было // [Ostrovki, E. Shedrovitsky, P. Russia: the country that has not been.]. Вестник СМИ 9(41) с. 2-6 [in Russian].

Ponsard, Lionel. 2007. *Russia, NATO, and Cooperative Security. Bridging the Gap.* Routledge.

Putin, Vladimir. 2001. "The speech on the Congress of Compatriots." 11 October. http://en.kremlin.ru/events/president/transcripts/21359 Accessed 12 October 2016.

Rannut, Mart. 2004. "Language Policy in Estonia." *Noves SL.. Revista de Sociolingüística,* Spring–Summer. http://www6.gencat.net/llengcat/noves/hm04primavera-estiu/docs/rannut.pdf. Accessed 28 August 2017.

Raun, Toivo. 2001. *Estonia and the Estonians.* Updated Second Edition. Stanford University: Hoover Institution Press.

RT. 2016. "Путин: граница России нигде не заканчивается." [Putin: the Border of Russia does not end anywhere]. RT [in Russian]. https://russian.rt.com/russia/news/335286-putin-grania-rossii Accessed 28 August 2017.

Rudensky, Nikolai. 1994. "Russian Minorities in the Newly Independent States. An International Problem in the Domestic Context of Russia Today." In *National Identity and Ethnicity in Russia and the New States of Eurasia*, edited by Roman Szporluk. M.E.Sharpe.

Saarpoll OÜ. 2015. "Elust, Usust ja Usuelust." ["On Life, Faith, and Faith Life"]. Saarpoll OÜ [in Estonian]. http://www.saarpoll.ee/UserFiles/File/Elus,%20usust%20ja%20usuelust_2015_ESITLUS_FINAL.pdf. Accessed 01 December 2018.

Schmidt, Royal J. 1956. "Cultural Nationalism in Herder." *Journal of the History of Ideas* Vol. 17(3): 407–417.

Transparency International. 2017. "Corruption Perceptions Index 2016."

https://www.transparency.org/news/feature/corruption_perceptions_index_2016 Accessed 07 November 2017.

Tsygankov, Andrei P. 2006. *Russia's Foreign Policy. Change and Continuity in National Identity*. Rowman and Littlefield Publishers, Inc.

Vihalemm, Peeter and Marju Lauristin, Veronika Kalmus, Triin Vihalemm, eds. 2017. *Eesti ühiskond kiirenevas ajas. Uuringu "Mina. Maailm. Meedia." 2002-2014 tulemused. [Estonian Society in the Changing Times. The results of the Survey "Me. World. Media."]*. Tartu ülikool [in Estonian].

10

Civilizational Perspectives in International Relations and Contemporary China-India Relations

RAVI DUTT BAJPAI

The end of the Cold War is considered one of the most critical episodes in world politics that restructured the global order from a bipolar world to a multipolar order, divided along ethnic, cultural and religious lines. The concept of civilizations reappeared in the discipline of International Relations (IR) at this time, with the publication and subsequent debates centered on 'The Clash of Civilizations' by Samuel Huntington (1993) which predicted a world order based on different and antagonistic civilizations. The fundamental assumption made under the 'clash of civilizations' hypothesis is that civilizations can be differentiated, based upon the fundamental incompatibility of beliefs, values and cultural norms among different civilizations. This 'clash of civilizations' hypothesis was challenged by several leading scholars. However, the terror attacks of 11 September 2001 and subsequent wars in Afghanistan and Iraq were construed as an endorsement of the 'clash of civilizations' hypothesis (Kapustin 2009). Huntington's theory, contentious as it is, continues to occupy a prominent position in contemporary IR discourses. This is underlined by a number of commemorative publications marking different anniversaries of Huntington's thesis (Barker 2013; Rose 2013).

Huntington has been critiqued primarily for being reductionist and essentialist in his understanding of civilizational identities; most critics have focused upon deconstructing the US-Islam dyad (Adib-Moghaddam 2010; Lyons 2014). I argue that, Huntington's classification of the Chinese civilization, the Hindu civilization and the Eastern civilization as distinct categories, in particular, clearly ignores the historical as well as contemporary affinities and inter-connectedness between these civilizations. Contrary to Huntington's reductionist view, IR has had a limited engagement with the legacy of peaceful and enriching interactions between the Chinese and Indian civilizations.

This paper explores the assumptions of civilizational identities purely based on cultural, religious or geographical distinctions and their limitations. It reviews the 'civilizations' discourse in IR and discusses the concept of 'civilization-states' in the context of China and India. It analyzes the key components of civilizational overlaps and exchanges between these two countries and the invocation of their 'civilization-state' identity in their contemporary bilateral relations. Rejecting Huntington's 'clash of civilizations' hypothesis in understanding 'civilization-states' like China and India, I conclude that it is critical to understand how states perceive their civilizational heritage, which both facilitates and impedes bilateral exchanges and the conduct of international relations.

Whither Civilizations in IR?

IR's engagement with civilizations coincided with fundamental changes in the global order which ushered decolonization, globalization and the end of the Cold War. A civilization is considered the largest and highest socio-historical phenomenon, and consists of numerous, diverse and distinct cultures within itself (Dawson 1970). The emergence of the concept of civilizations in IR, goes beyond Huntington's 'clash of civilizations' and has led to the focus on how and why different civilizational identities have distinct worldviews. As Bettiza describes, 'Civilizations are socially constructed when people somewhere not only identify themselves but are also recognized by others as either the archetypal representatives of a civilization' (2014, 19). Martin Hall underlines the advent of civilizational identities in IR and argues that, 'civilizational analysis is important not least because the concept of civilization is being used'. It seems, 'at this historical juncture, that the notion of civilization is a significant carrier of knowledge and of thereby attendant preferences and policies' (Hall 2007, 199). Nevertheless, how do civilizations acquire political meaning and character?

As social collectives, civilizations represent 'imagined communities' similar to nation-states, however, civilizations are manifestly distinct to nation-states, both in temporal and spatial dimensions. This implies that unlike nation-states, civilizations exist at sub-national and supranational levels and therefore, civilizations may be deployed in IR to represent 'transnational, inter-human, and de-territorialized cultural communities' (Bettiza 2014, 4).

This expanse of geographical and social diversity implies that civilizations encompass several distinctive constituents and are in a constant state of flux within themselves.

Civilizations undergo changes both from their internal diversity and from inter-civilizational encounters (Cox 2000, 220). Unlike the rigid territorial boundaries of nation-states, civilizations spill over national borders and defy territoriality and boundaries. The inter-civilizational interactions are ubiquitous; Europe's progress to a 'modern' civilization was assisted by such exchanges with China, India, and the Islamic world (Arnason 2006). These inter-civilizational interactions assume political significance when civilizations are deployed as discursive practices for identity construction. Civilizational identity may be used to define the boundaries of a community by differentiating between self and the other; it can also be used to locate the self at the global, regional, or individual levels and also to evaluate others.

China and India at the institutional-state and individual-citizen levels have deployed the narratives of their glorious past to progress from not-so-glorious present to potentially glorious future. The histories for both China and India are not in museums, artefacts and archaeological specimens but in their visions of the thriving magnificence of their civilizational glories. However, it is not enough merely to claim an identity; that identity must have a degree of social effectiveness and political purchase and others must acknowledge the identity itself as legitimate. China and India both claim the status of rightful inheritors of their ancient civilizations; while these claims are not completely uncontested, they have general recognition in the society of nations. So what is the political salience of their civilizational heritage?

China and India: 'State' of the Civilizations

Civilizational entitlement allows states to consider themselves as the natural and worthy inheritors of their ancient civilizational glories, and frame policies to regain the power and status befitting of 'their country's size, population, geographic position and historical heritage' (Malik 2011, 28). The civilizational legacies of China and India not only continue to define the national identities of the two states, but also set the background for the bilateral relations between them. There are remarkable similarities in the construction of Chinese and Indian national identities as modern nation-states; both frame their national identities in terms of civilizational entitlement and colonial occupation (Malik 2011).

This sense of entitlement is further entrenched in the national identity construction, as foreign occupation is held responsible for the loss of ancient civilizational grandeurs and status. The colonial control not only interrupted traditional approaches to statecraft and international interactions based upon Chinese and Indian civilizational attributes, but it also altered the Chinese and Indian perceptions about the glories of their own civilizations (Sheel 2007). These civilizational attributes in China and India were derived from a combination of history, geography and culture. The geographical perspective accorded the population in the respective areas later identified as China and India, with a sense of cultural affinity among themselves. The old maritime and caravan routes facilitated the diffusion of trade, culture and religion among the Chinese, Indians and the rest of Asia. These cultural and material exchanges led to an international order based upon mutual reciprocity rather than absolute power or control.

Tan Chung refers to this mutually beneficial interaction and the collaborative framework between China and India as 'geo-civilizational' rather than a 'geopolitical' paradigm. It is quite extraordinary that despite the geographical proximity, unlike other Western civilizations, the Chinese and Indian civilizations have enjoyed peaceful and mutually enriching relations for over twenty centuries until the Cold War period. Chung (2009, 211) underlines this paradox, 'it was during the Cold War that the two new republics were born and have paid heavy tuition fees to learn international politics'. A vibrant cultural, commercial and political relationship was blossoming between the two civilizations prior to the Christian era and was reflected in exchanges in diverse fields such as agriculture, science, mathematics, astronomy literature, linguistics, architecture and medicine (Sen 2004).

The postcolonial states of China and India adopted the idea of victimhood as an essential part of national identity construction, referred to as 'the century of national humiliation' in China and 'a century of rule by an alien race and culture' in India (Garver 2011, 103). China and India both claim to be victims of extractive colonialism and this sense of victimhood shapes their contemporary international relations objectives of protecting absolute sovereignty and reclaiming their international prestige. In the case of both China and India the national identity construction is sustained from the entitlement of glorious civilizational heritage.

The construction of the national and civilizational identities is a multi-layered process that involves several competing frames of political, cultural, social and ethnic affiliations. These different affiliations often overlap and some of the characteristics used in this process of identity construction are shared between China and India. This is not to claim that both societies adopt exactly the same attributes in the construction of their civilizational identity; rather to highlight the differences in the definition and deployment of these characteristics. Generally, national identity is associated with political representation while civilizational identity denotes cultural affiliations. However, in the case of China and India the national and civilizational identities are considered interchangeable, and both of these identities have acquired political connotations.

China and India share a common civilizational heritage largely through Buddhism, which may be considered as a coherent cultural complex, in a much broader sense than a civilization. In this case, Buddhism does not override the distinct civilizational identities contained within it. It is not the whole but one constituent element of the larger structure of the Chinese and Indian civilizations. The spread of Buddhism to China brought certain Indian cultural elements into China, and in due course, some of these distinctly Indian elements became part of the Chinese civilization. Sinicized Buddhism thrived alongside Confucianism and Daoism. It appears that while Buddhism as a shared inter-civilizational heritage may provide for greater convergence between China and India, it is now also portrayed as another avenue for sustaining the rivalry. The phenomenon of 'faith diplomacy' as a tool of international relations has gained prominence in recent times and both China and India have deployed Buddhism in their soft power diplomacy and cultural outreach, specifically in dealing with Central and Southeast Asian states (Scott 2016).

In contemporary times China has preferred to deploy its Buddhist legacies as a diplomatic resource rather than deploying other cultural or philosophical traditions. Juyan Zhang claims that the Chinese state considers both Confucianism and Buddhism to have inherent 'Chineseness' (2013, 85). China is keen to promote its version of Buddhism and Tibetan figures such as the Panchen Lama, to counterbalance the global appeal of the Dalai Lama. China realizes the importance of Buddhism's soft-power capabilities especially in the context of smaller Buddhist countries in Asia. As Juyan Zhang contends, 'China would have fully employed Taoism if it were an internationalized religion' (2013, 92).

Buddhism cannot be the only singular narrative of the civilizational heritage that frames China and India's national and international policies. Some useful inferences can be made from the behavioral trends of the two countries at the domestic and international levels. India projects its civilizational status as 'domestically tolerant and pluralistic, and externally non-aggressive and non-interventionist' (Ollapally 2014). India's international exchanges have been based on religious-philosophical ideas, cultures, and trade. China derives its civilizational status from humanist values, homogeneity and uniformity and externally on the idea of the 'Middle Kingdom' of cultural and material superiority over the outside world (Scott 2007, 10). Both China and India's international exchanges have been based on creating order, gaining prestige, maintaining dignity and achieving suzerainty rather than territorial occupation in the immediate neighborhood.

It is significant to highlight that at the time of their birth as new nation-states both China and India were considered too fragile to stand on their own; their economy, internal security and external defense were considered to be vulnerable. It is quite remarkable that despite their limitations both China and India pursued independent foreign policies instead of bandwagoning with one of the superpowers in the bipolar world. This independent approach to foreign policy in China and India was a result of their adverse experiences with colonial powers but it was also driven by their strategic cultures. This strategic culture was grounded in China and India's self-perception of being civilization-state rather than just former 'empire-states' or modern day 'nation-states' (Malik 2011, 28).

In 1954, China and India adopted 'Five Principles' (*Pancha Sila*) as the foundational framework of their bilateral interactions; it was an illustrative example of deploying the civilizational heritage to conduct international interactions. A Communist China under an atheistic Mao and a secular India under an averred non-religious Nehru adopted *Pancha Sila*, primarily a Buddhist concept. The Chinese Communist Party's aversion to ritualistic religions has been well known while India after its partition on religious lines had proclaimed to profess secularism as its national identity. However, both China and India engaged in invoking an essentially religious system to guide their bilateral relationship. It is significant to underline Mao's interpretation of Buddhism not in religious but cultural terms; 'in Mao's eyes, Daoism and Buddhism are all cultures, even excellent cultures' (Fang 2014, 327).

China and India could have invoked other concepts such as their postcolonial status, the idea of a pan-Asian camaraderie, developing world solidarity or some other mutually inclusive construct towards a cohesive and shared world view. The heritage of two ancient civilizations allowed both China and India to venture beyond the strictly nation-state based secular boundaries and accommodate some form of the religious system in their bilateral relations. *Pancha Sila* was one such example of assimilating contradictions between the nation-state and the civilizational heritage. The official policies of both the Chinese and Indian states were firmly tied to the secular ideals but a religious philosophical idea was used to promote bilateral cooperation. It can be claimed that in this case the civilizational heritage, prevailed over state-centric thinking (Chacko 2013). The complex nature of the self-identity espoused by the Chinese and Indians is that of a 'civilization state' which is discussed in the next section.

China and India: 'Civilization-States'

The process of modern nation-state formation in the Westphalian order ignored various pre-modern and non-European models of the state and the existence of dynamic societies like China and India. A 'civilization-state' can be considered a political configuration similar to a 'nation state'; however, while civilizations may be considered 'imagined communities' they are not represented by governments and additionally they do not have formal representatives (Bettiza 2014, 14). Civilizations are made up of ethnic groups who share a common geographic locus and a common set of values with a shared history, shared culture, and shared socio-political institutions. A civilization may be seen as a conglomeration of a variety of peoples or ethnic groups, continuation from ancient periods, social and cultural practices and also vast spaces (Wei 2012). In such a formulation, civilization can be interpreted as an enlarged 'nation-state'. As a comparative example, Europe with an assortment of cultures, religions, ethnic groups, languages and vernacular diversity, can be considered one civilization, and in this context both modern India and modern China can be perceived as civilization-states (Jacques 2012).

It is important to highlight that, like civilization, the concept of 'civilization-state' also has a postcolonial context. In their quest to be considered a civilized nation, several countries in Asia strived hard to emulate the institutions, practices, social norms and legal-political lexicon of their European conquerors; Japan and Turkey may be considered as the frontrunners of this trend (Duara 2001, 101). The discourses on the right for self-rule and anti-colonial movements in the colonies were framed in such a way that it was imagined that these countries could progress from uncivilized or half-civilized to civilized societies. The self-proclamation of being inheritors to ancient civilizations was one of the fundamental arguments to promote the idea of nationalism during the anti-colonial movements. Arguably, in contemporary times nationalists are able to deploy civilization as a supplement to nationalism (Duara 2001).

The association between nationalism, state and ancient civilizational histories should be seen in the context of how the right to statehood and the right to own history were interwoven during the periods of colonization (Bowden 2009). German philosopher Hegel equated history to statehood and claimed, 'people or a nation lacked history . . . not because it knew no writing but because lacking as it did in statehood it had nothing to write about' (Hegel cited in Bowden 2009, 79). In this context Hegel writes about India and its lack of history by claiming that 'Hindoos have no History in the form of annals (*historia*) that they have no History in the form of transactions (*res gestæ*); that is, no growth expanding into a veritable political condition' (Hegel 2001, 181). Ranajit Guha, describes this process of inclusion and exclusion in world history and claims that the narrative of civilization shifted from 'no writing, no history, to no state, no history' (Guha 2002, 10). In such a diverse understanding of civilization and states, how do we understand the trajectory of China and India as 'civilization-states' that have mutually coexisted over centuries?

Lucian Pye designated China as a 'civilization pretending to be a nation-state' (1992, 232). Pye's assessment had negative connotations as he juxtaposed the state controlled Chinese polity against the normative Western-centric concept of the modern liberal state. The role of the 'civilization-state' in the Chinese political system was highlighted by Tu Wei-ming, who claimed that 'the civilization-state exercises both political power and moral influence' (1991, 16). However, Tu Wei-ming lamented the marginalization of China from the global order, 'It should be acknowledged, however, that for all her power and influence, China as a civilization-state is often negligible in the international discourse on global human concerns' (1991, 16). The subsequent two decades witnessed China's rapid rise to global leadership, coupled with China's renewed interest in framing its international relations discourse on its unique civilizational heritage. The advent of Xi Jinping as the Chinese president in 2012 propelled the idea of 'civilization-state' to the forefront of the political discourse; as Xi believed that 'a civilization carries on its back the soul of a country or nation' (2014).

China can be considered a civilization-state based on its long and uninterrupted history, enormous geography, massive population, diverse demography, the continuity of traditions and cultural systems, and finally the incorporation of many 'Chinas' within one core political unit. The enduring influences of Confucian and Buddhist values in China, in one or the other form over a long period of history, make the Chinese civilization unique among all the ancient civilizations. Another defining feature of the Chinese civilization is its long-running existence as a political unit, since 221 BC when the first Chinese imperial state was founded (Gernet 1996). The landmass referred to as the Chinese heartland has remained under the control of one polity (Gamer 2012). China claims to follow the 'one country, two systems' formula in dealing with Hong Kong; such an approach would be impractical for a typical nation-state. As a modern state, China has been ruled by several different political ideologies: rigid Marxism during Mao's period, soft Socialism under Deng Xiaoping and then aggressive but state controlled Capitalism in the post Deng period. China's imminent collapse has been predicted on several occasions, post-Cold War, post-Tiananmen Square massacre, and post-Global Financial Crisis. It appears that China defies all the conventional frameworks of an archetypical nation-state in the post-Westphalian system.

Although India has not been classified as a 'civilization-state' in IR discourses, the case for India to be considered a 'civilization-state' is equally strong based on the attributes such as an uninterrupted history, the size of the geographical area and population, diversity of the demographics and above all the continuity of traditional cultural systems. India was shown as a landmass of hundreds of small to medium princely states rather than one political unit at the advent of the British Empire. On the other hand, it can be claimed that despite the lack of political unity, the cultural similarities among these states made them a part of one broad civilizational collective (Desai 2009).

However, India differs from China in three aspects. Unlike the dominance of Confucianism in China's polity and society, India does not have one dominant school of thought; rather, it has inherited several diverse and often contradictory philosophical traditions. India's demographic diversity is much broader than China's and while 79% of the Indian population is classified as Hindus, there is no singular cultural-religious-ideational criteria that can amalgamate Hindus as one unit. The multiplicity of racial, ethnic, linguistic and religious identities makes India more of a subcontinent than a unified nation-state. Unlike China, post-independent India has largely followed one type of governance structure, that of parliamentary democracy through regular electoral mandates. India has adopted an approach similar to 'one country, two systems' employed in China, with the state of Jammu and Kashmir.

Although India's ancient civilizational legacy originates from its Hindu-Buddhist religious beliefs, the constitutional secularism in the Indian polity makes it difficult for the state to flaunt a religious identity. While Indian political leaders have refrained from a public display of its civilizational heritage there has always been a palpable sense of this heritage in the Indian public and policy circles. References to India's ancient civilizational heritage are often made by the ruling elite both for national and international audiences (Michael 2013, 36). Prime Minister Modi's recent policy announcements and speeches are appropriate examples of how he often draws from ancient thinkers and traditions that define 'Indianness'. While India may be reticent to display its civilizational heritage in the international arena, India has never been taciturn about invoking its historically civilizational associations with China.

The self-perception of China and India as civilization-states has also led to greater competition to enhance their international prestige and power projections relative to each other. In their bilateral interactions, China and India emphasize Buddhism to achieve greater cooperation, while both also deploy Buddhism to gain greater influence in Central and Southeast Asia. The genesis of the 1962 border war and the ongoing territorial disputes between China and India lie with this divergent self-perception of being a civilization-state. Subsequent to the Chinese takeover of Tibet, India provided sanctuary to the Dalai Lama – a move that made India highly suspect in China's eyes. India's move to provide sanctuary to the Dalai Lama was not entirely a political decision nor was India in any viable position to contest China in Tibet. China misconstrued the depth of reverence for the Dalai Lama in India; the spiritual and religious foundations of Indian civilization considers Tibetan Buddhism as a part of their own heritage. The Indian state and particularly Prime Minister Nehru on their part misconstrued China's determination to reinstate their earlier preeminence in the emerging regional order. These contestations between India and China are a dominant feature of their different and competing claims to civilizational legacies.

Conclusion

There seems to be a consensus among various scholars that India and China, as key actors in emerging Asia, are simultaneously moving upward on relative power trajectories while sustaining a rivalry which will further magnify. The references to the 'clash of civilizations' hypothesis in the context of China and India have been framed in the familiar geopolitical perspective, rather than through their histories of civilizational exchanges. China and India are considered civilizational twins as well as eternal rivals. It is clear that the civilizational narrative is never too distanced in their exchanges, be it towards a grand harmony, international alliances, cold peace or outright war. To conclude, the discipline of International Relations has much to gain from inter-civilizational perspectives which are integral to understanding the behavior of 'civilization-states' in non-Western contexts. Any purposeful analysis of the China-India bilateral relationship and their worldviews, in particular, is not possible without studying their inter-civilizational links.

References

Adib-Moghaddam, Arshin. 2010. *A Metahistory of the Clash of Civilizations: Us and Them Beyond Orientalism*. New York: Columbia University Press.

Arnason, Johann P. 2006. "Understanding Intercivilizational Encounters." *Thesis Eleven* 86(1): 39–53. https://doi.org/10.1177/0725513606066239

Barker, J. Paul, ed. 2013. *The Clash of Civilizations: Twenty Years On*. Bristol, UK: E-International Relations. http://www.e-ir.info/wp-content/uploads/Clash-of-Civilizations-E-IR.pdf

Bettiza, Gregorio. 2014. "Civilizational Analysis in International Relations: Mapping the Field and Advancing a 'Civilizational Politics' Line of Research." *International Studies Review* 16(1): 1–28. https://doi.org/10.1111/misr.12100

Bowden, Brett. 2009. "Inter-civilizational Relations: Past, Present, Future." Paper presented at International Studies Association 2009 Annual Convention, New York.

Chacko, Priya. 2013. *Indian Foreign Policy: The Politics of Postcolonial Identity from 1947 to 2004*. London and New York: Routledge.

Chung, Tan. 2009. "Historical Chindian Paradigm Inter-cultural Transfusion and Solidification." *China Report* 45(3): 187–212.

Cox, Robert W. 2000. "Thinking About Civilizations." *Review of International Studies* 26(5): 217–234.

Dawson, Christopher. 1970. *Progress and Religion: A Historical Enquiry*. Westport: Greenwood Press.

Desai, Meghnad. 2009. *The Rediscovery of India*. New Delhi: Penguin Books India.

Duara, Prasenjit. 2001. "The Discourse of Civilization and Pan-Asianism." Journal of World History 12(1): 99–130.

Fang, Litian. 2014. "On the Sinicized Marxist View of Religion." In *Marxism and Religion*, edited by Z Chi, X Gong and D Lü, 321–347. Leiden and The Netherlands: Brill.

Gamer, Robert E. 2012. *Understanding Contemporary China*. 4th Ed. Boulder: Lynne Rienner Publishers.

Garver, John. 2011. "The Unresolved Sino–Indian Border Dispute." *China Report* 47(2): 99–113. https://doi.org/10.1177/000944551104700204

Gernet, Jacques. 1996. *A History of Chinese Civilization*. Cambridge, UK: Cambridge University Press.

Guha, Ranajit. 2002. *History at the Limit of World-history, Italian Academy Lectures*. New York: Columbia University Press.

Hall, Martin. 2007. "Toward a Fourth Generation in Civilizational Scholarship." In *Civilizational Identity: The Production and Reproduction of 'Civilizations' In International Relations*, edited by Martin Hall and Patrick Thaddeus Jackson, 199–205. New York: Palgrave Macmillan.

Hegel, Georg Wilhelm Friedrich. 2001. *The Philosophy of History*. Kitchener: Batoche Books.

Huntington, Samuel P. 1993. "The Clash of Civilizations?" *Foreign affairs* 72(3): 22–49.

Jacques, Martin. 2012. *When China Rules The World: The Rise of The Middle Kingdom and The End of The Western World*. New York: Penguin Books.

Kapustin, Boris. 2009. "Some Political Meanings of 'Civilization.'" *Diogenes* 56(2–3): 151–169.

Lyons, Jonathan. 2014. *Islam through Western Eyes: From the Crusades to the War on Terrorism*. New York; Chichester: Columbia University Press.

Malik, Mohan. 2011. *China and India: Great Power Rivals*. Boulder: FirstForumPress.

Michael, Arndt. 2013. *India's Foreign Policy and Regional Multilateralism*. Basingstoke: Palgrave Macmillan.

Ollapally, Deepa M. 2014. "India's Evolving National Identity Contestation: What Reactions to the 'Pivot' Tell Us." *The ASAN Forum*, 25 January. http://www.theasanforum.org/indias-evolving-national-identity-contestation-what-reactions-to-the-pivot-tell-us/

Pye, Lucian W. 1992. *The Spirit of Chinese Politics*. Cambridge, MA: Harvard University Press.

Rose, Gideon, ed. 2013. *Foreign Affairs Collection: The Clash at 20*. Tampa: Foreign Affairs. http://home.sogang.ac.kr/sites/jaechun/courses/Lists/b6/Attachments/9/clash of civilization.pdf

Scott, David. 2007. *China Stands Up: The PRC and The International System*. London and New York: Routledge.

Scott, David. 2016. "Buddhism in Current China-India Diplomacy." *Journal of Current Chinese Affairs* 45(3): 139–174.

Sen, Amartya. 2004. "Passage to China." *New York Review of Books* 51: 61–63.

Sheel, Kamal. 2007. "China's Changing Discourse on India." *Seminar* 573: 43–48.

Wei-ming, Tu. 1991. "Cultural China: the periphery as the center." *Daedalus* 134(4): 145–167.

Wei, Ruan. 2012. "Two Concepts of 'Civilization.'" *Comparative Civilizations Review* (67): 16–26.

Xi, Jinping. 2014. "Speech by HE Xi Jinping President of the People's Republic of China at UNESCO Headquarters." *Ministry of Foreign Affairs of PRC*. http://www.fmprc.gov.cn/mfa_eng/wjdt_665385/zyjh_665391/t1142560.shtml

Zhang, Juyan. 2013. "China's Faith Diplomacy." In *Religion and Public Diplomacy*, edited by Philip Seib, 75–98. New York: Palgrave Macmillan.

11

The 'Clash of Civilizations' in International Law

WOUTER WERNER

Clashing Disciplines

Sometimes international law and international relations are two worlds apart. When Samuel Huntington published his article and book 'The Clash of Civilizations' in 1993 and 1997, it made quite a splash in the field of International Relations. The piece was discussed and critiqued intensively at the time, and as this special issue attests, after more than 20 years his work is still considered worth discussing, exploring and critiquing. On the other side of the disciplinary divide, things looked quite different. While Huntington's thesis was certainly noticed in international law (Rehman 2005), his impact on international scholarship more broadly was modest, to say the least. References to Huntington's work are often made more in passing and generally not with the aim of a serious engagement with his work.[1] Conversely, international law is almost completely neglected in Huntington's work. It is hardly mentioned at all, apart from incidental remarks such as 'Western law coming out of the tradition of Grotius' (Huntington 1997, 52) (without explaining what this entails exactly) or it is equated with Western ideas about governance and human rights.

In this (brief) article, I will focus on the possible contribution of international law to the debates and critiques on the 'clash of civilizations'. More particularly, I will argue that a more in-depth engagement with international law would enrich the debate on the 'clash of civilizations' for at least two reasons.

---

[1]   See for example Miller and Bratspies (2008, 9 and 10), where the editors move from a brief mention of Huntington's thesis straight to a discussion of the functional fragmentation of international law.

The 'Clash of Civilizations' in International Law

First, international law could help to explore the performative effects of claims about 'clashing civilizations'. For Huntington, the thesis of the 'clash of civilizations' is meant as a diagnosis of the post-Cold War world; as an explanatory frame that competes with other approaches in International Relations such as realism.[2] In other words: Huntington presents his claim as if it deals with an object that is external to it. However, it is difficult to maintain this strict separation, especially if the speaker is part of the society that (s)he describes. In that case, statements about the 'nature' of a society come with normative consequences. For example, for someone who conceives of one's society as composed of egoistic individuals, the normative ties to others are different than for someone who holds that society is rooted in common fate and pride.[3] Somewhat paradoxically, this insight is at the heart of Huntington's diagnoses of different civilizations, but it is not applied to his own position.

For (international) lawyers, going back and forth between descriptive and performative aspects of 'society' is quite common. Take for example the structure of the (in)famous 1927 *Lotus* judgment of the Permanent Court of International Justice (PCIJ). The PCIJ was called to decide whether Turkey enjoyed jurisdiction to try a French officer who failed his duty to prevent a collision between a French and a Turkish ship on the high seas. In order to answer this question, the PCIJ postulated what it regarded as the nature of international legal society at the time: 'International law governs relations between independent states'. From this characterization it followed, according to the Court, that 'the rules of law binding upon states therefore emanate from their own free will (....); restrictions upon the independence of states cannot therefore be presumed' (Lotus case [1927], p18). In other words, the concept of 'society' functioned as an institutional fact, linking the apparent 'is' of the existence of sovereign states to the 'ought' of their legal freedoms. The case of *Lotus* is just one example of courts and tribunals postulating the nature of (international) society as the foundation of normative ties existing between the members of that society.[4]

Secondly, international law seems an obvious starting point to reflect on clashing civilizations. After all, modern international law was to a large extent born out of such clashes, and developed into a system that defined and stratified 'civilizations' for centuries. One of the core questions that occupied the minds of early modern thinkers in international law concerned the treatment of radically different civilizations by European, colonizing powers.

---

[2]   See for example Huntington's description of what counts as a sound model at (Huntington 1997, 30).

[3]   For an elaborate analysis of the impact of different conceptions of society and the rule of law see Dworkin (1985).

[4]   For an analysis see Werner (2016). The part on the *Lotus* case is taken from this article.

As I will set out in section one, international law developed into one of the tools employed by colonial powers to label, categorize and manage differences and clashes between (postulated) civilizations. In section two I will set out how international law tried to overcome its colonial heritages in the twentieth century through the adoption of a protective conception of sovereignty as well as a core of cosmopolitan norms that were supposed to transcend nations and civilizations. The net result, as I will argue in section three, is that international law now offers possibilities to conceptualize world politics in radically different ways, including clashes of civilizations, relations between sovereigns and the regulation of issues of universal nature. Through a brief discussion of the controversies between the African Union and the International Criminal Court I will illustrate how these three are mobilized in concrete cases. Huntington's work functions as a reminder, and warning signal, that such mobilizations remain possible within international law. While it may be true that any invocation of 'civilization' rests on shaky empirical foundations, the consequences of such invocations are too real to be ignored.

From Vitoria to the Standard of Civilization

For modern international law, the idea that civilizations may clash goes back at least to the early 16th century. Just a cursory look at the title of one of the canonical texts of early modern international law shows how much the rise of international law had to do with civilizations in conflict. The reflections on the law of war by Francisco de Vitoria (1483–1546) bore the title, 'on the Indians; or the law of war made by the Spaniards on the barbarians'.[5] The core question informing Vitoria's teachings on the subject was whether the Spanish crown enjoyed the right to wage war upon a radically different, 'barbaric' civilization. While Vitoria is rightly praised for his critical and cosmopolitan ethos throughout, his work was also characterized by some core differentiations between European and Native American civilizations, and an obvious bias in favor of the right to travel, trade and preach on the part of the Spaniards.[6]

In the following centuries, international law only deepened the divisions between 'Western' and 'other' civilizations. Or, to be more precise: it more and more presented Europe/the West as 'civilized' and other parts of the world as either uncivilized or barbaric. The heyday of these differentiations was in the nineteenth and early twentieth century, when disciplines such as anthropology and ethnology provided an allegedly scientific basis for legal

---

[5]   The text can be found, *inter alia*, at 'Constitution Society'. Available at: http://www. constitution.org/victoria/victoria_5.htm Accessed 21 September 2017.

[6]   For an analysis see Anghie (2004). For an emphasis on Vitoria's cosmopolitan thinking, see Scott (1934).

differentiations between cultures. The British international lawyer Lorimer, for example, identified three concentric zones of humanity: civilized humanity, barbarous humanity and savage humanity; each with a descending level of legal recognition (2005, 101). Even when international lawyers voiced their concerns about the way in which the colonial enterprise was conducted and spoke out on behalf of colonized communities, it remained exceptional to find fundamental critiques of the idea that different stages of civilization came with different legal entitlements.[7] Legal relations between civilized powers were regulated by rules that were different from the rules that regulated the interaction with Islamic nations. As Wheaton (1836, 51) put it: 'The international law of the civilized, Christian nations of Europe and America, is one thing; and that which governs the intercourse with the Mohammedan nations of the East with each other and with the Christian, is another and very different thing'.[8] Relations between colonial powers and native communities remained largely outside the sphere of positive international law, and were governed by a core set of rules of natural law (to be interpreted and applied mainly by those in power). The club of 'civilized nations' was exclusive, but not completely closed. There was a possibility for newcomers to enter, if they managed to pass the so called 'standard of civilization' test, a rather indeterminate standard used by Western powers to negotiate their position vis-à-vis states such as Turkey or Japan.[9] Remnants of the idea that international law is a matter of 'civilized nations' can still be found in the Statute of the International Court of Justice, which is, according to article 38, empowered to apply the 'general principles of law recognized by civilized nations'.

This (too) brief historical sketch shows that the use of terms such as 'civilization' tends to come with stratifications and hierarchies. In the history of international law, 'civilization' has generally been invoked to create an inferior 'other' and to plea for unequal rights between the core and the periphery. While the use of terms such as 'civilization' came with a flavor of scientific objectivity, in fact it functioned as an ideological framework to justify structures of domination.

---

[7]   For an excellent analysis of the position of nineteenth century international lawyers in relation to colonialism see Koskenniemi (2002), in particular chapter two.

[8]   The quote is taken from Koskenniemi (2002, 115).

[9]   As Koskenniemi (2002, 135) has put it: 'The existence of a "standard" was a myth in the sense that there was never anything to gain. Every concession was a matter of negotiation, every status depended on agreement, *quid pro quo*. But the existence of a *language of a standard* still gave the appearance of a fair treatment (...)'. The classical study on the standard of civilization remains Gong (1984).

Clashes of Civilization in an Era of Formal Equality

Today, the invocation of 'civilizational differences' has not disappeared. Several authors, including Samuel Huntington[10], have argued that new standards of civilization have emerged in the name of human rights, security, democracy, rule of law or international trade and investment law.[11] Interestingly however, most of the time, such references to reborn 'standards of civilization' are made to *critique* the direction of international law. The underlying assumption is mostly that equality between nations and cultures should be the norm, but alas, international law is still far removed from this ideal. In other words: if someone argues that something like a 'standard of civilization' drives a legal regime, this is almost invariably done in an attempt to show the illegitimacy of the regime in question; not to justify it.[12]

This turn-around reflects an important development in international law more generally. In the course of the twentieth century, the formal division of the world into spheres of civilization was replaced by a new interpretation of what sovereign equality of nations entailed. International law rapidly changed its stand towards colonialism, arguing for a right to self-determination of colonized peoples instead.[13] Newly independent states born out of decolonization were protected by a conception of sovereignty that differed significantly from its nineteenth century counterpart. Sovereignty no longer meant the prerogative to decide when it was necessary to wage war, but instead meant that states were formally protected against intervention and the use of force by their peers.[14] In other words: sovereignty moved from a freedom to wage war towards a freedom against armed interventions (Aalberts & Werner, 2008). At the same time, post-1945 international law adopted norms with universal pretensions to an unprecedented degree, e.g. in the form of human rights law, regimes to protect areas such as Antarctica or outer space, or norms regulating behavior in times of armed conflict. These norms claim to go beyond the specific interests of states or the values held by

---

[10]   Although Huntington does not explicitly link his invocation of the imperialist heritage to international law, his line of argumentation is similar to that of several critical legal scholars: 'The West is attempting and will continue to attempt to sustain its preeminent position and defend its interests by defining those interests as the interests of the "world community"' (1997, 184).

[11]   The classical work in this respect remains Anghie (2004). See also Douzinas (2007).

[12]   Infra note 15.

[13]   The landmark Resolutions driving this process were General Assembly Resolutions 1514 (1960) and 2625 (1970). For an analysis of decolonization and specific aspects of international law see Craven (2009).

[14]   For an analysis of the significance of this changing conception of sovereignty see Schmitt (2003).

different cultures. Instead, they are meant to protect interests of humankind as such, or to embody values that make it possible for nations and cultures to co-exist in the first place.

This is not to say that formal equality between sovereigns or the protection of individual rights and communal interests has completely set aside the logic of civilizational differences. International law is also still characterized by formalized inequalities between states and regions in the world, e.g. in the composition of the Security Council or the distribution of voting rights in some international forums (Simpson 2004). In addition, the application of universal norms is still affected by unequal power relations, so that some states are more likely to be called to account for violations of international norms than others. As a result, international law today offers different normative vocabularies that can be mobilized to conceptualize political struggles and societal problems. Alongside the vocabularies of formal sovereignty and universal values, there is a vocabulary of empire and domination of one 'civilization' over another. As I argued in the first section, the use of such vocabularies should not be treated (only) as if they are truth claims. They are also presentations of the nature of international relations, including the presentation of its main subjects and the normative ties that exist between those subjects. In the last section I will illustrate the mobilization of competing presentations of international society through a discussion of the struggles between the African Union and the International Criminal Court.

The International Criminal Court and 'Africa'

According to Huntington in 1996, Africa possessed a weak civilizational identity at best. He added, however, 'Africans are also developing a sense of African identity, and conceivably sub-Saharan Africa could cohere into a distinct civilization, with South Africa possibly being its core state' (Huntington 1997 47).

Whatever one may think of the descriptive and predictive value of both statements, attempts at developing an African identity have been made by diplomatic elites since the end of the Cold War. In this context, the International Criminal Court (ICC) has proven a useful point of reference to develop such an identity. Initially, the ICC fitted well in the change of identity that came with the death of the Organization of African States (OAS) and the birth of its replacement, the African Union (AU). Where the OAS revolved around issues of decolonization and adopted non-intervention as the core principle among African states, the African Union openly embraced, at least formally, constitutional government, democracy and human rights and allowed for intervention in cases of unconstitutional changes in government or gross human rights violations.[15] The African Union thus was more than a practical arrangement between states; it also constituted an attempt to redefine the nature of the relations between African states and peoples. In line with this ethos, more than 30 African states decided to join the newly established International Criminal Court (ICC).

At first sight, the ICC has a clear cosmopolitan outlook, epitomized by its commitment to fight crimes that 'deeply shock the consciousness of humanity', 'threaten the peace, security and well-being of the world' and deserve to be prosecuted by 'every State' (Preamble to the Rome Statute of the ICC). The ICC, in other words, operates on the assumption that the world is bound together by certain core values, or as the preamble to the ICC Statute describes it, the assumption that 'all peoples are united by common bonds, their cultures pieced together in a shared heritage'. From this imagery of international relations follows an obligation for all states to prosecute crimes that threaten the 'delicate mosaic' that holds the world together, and to accept the power of the ICC to step in if states are unwilling or unable to do so. The language of a global community united against 'enemies of mankind' was mobilized, *inter alia*, by the government of Uganda after it referred the situation in Northern Uganda to the ICC. Its long-standing fight against the Lord's Resistance Army could now be articulated as a fight against enemies of the word as a whole, backed up by a cosmopolitan institution (Nouwen and Werner 2010).

However, despite its cosmopolitan outlook the ICC is also an organization that rests on the will and cooperation of sovereign states. Earlier international criminal tribunals were often created top-down, by victorious powers (e.g. Nuremberg, Tokyo) or by the Security Council (e.g. Yugoslavia, Rwanda). The ICC is created bottom-up, through a treaty that rests on the freely expressed consent of sovereign states. This of course seriously hampers the cosmopolitan ambitions of the ICC, as is evidenced by the absence – and lack of cooperation – of powerful states such as the United States, China or Russia. The ICC not only rests on a treaty created by and through the consent of states, it also heavily depends on states when it comes to the effectuation of its arrest warrants. Since the ICC lacks its own police force, it can only serve its cosmopolitan agenda if states are willing and able to cooperate with the ICC.

---

[15]   See in particular article four of the Constitutive Act of the African Union. After reaffirming the principles of sovereign equality and non-intervention, the Act empowers the Union to interfere when war crimes, genocide and crimes against humanity are committed, and emphasizes respect for democratic principles, human rights, the rule of law and good governance.

The ICC is thus a cosmopolitan and a state-centric organization at the same time. Both aspects are symbolized by article 13 of the ICC Statute, which regulates the conditions under which the Court may exercise its jurisdiction. According to article 13, the Court may exercise jurisdiction if a state party refers a case to the ICC, thus laying the initiative in the hands of governments of sovereign states. Another option offered by article 13 is that the Prosecutor initiates proceedings, thus empowering one of the organs of the Court itself. However, there is a third way in which proceedings can kick off, and that is if the Security Council refers a situation to the Court. In effect, this means that the (permanent) members of the Security Council enjoy special powers to determine which situations the Court can take up. The position of the members of the Council is further strengthened by article 16 of the Statute. According to this article, the Security Council can block investigations or prosecutions by the ICC for a period of 12 months, and offers the Council the opportunity to renew the request under the same conditions. This brings a third image of the Court: the Court as an institution rooted in legalized inequality between the permanent members of the Security Council and the rest of the world.

The ICC thus offers an interesting illustration of three different vocabularies on the nature of the legal community it regulates: a cosmopolitan narrative, a narrative of sovereign equality and a narrative of formal inequality. All three have been mobilized lately by several African states and the African Union in their critiques of the ICC. Put simply, the critique is that the ICC has focused almost exclusively on African situations, as if the most heinous criminals all reside on this continent. The cosmopolitan symbolism of the ICC is thus recognized, but turned against the ICC itself: precisely because the ICC claims to deal with crimes that shock the conscience of humanity, it should be careful not to locate these crimes exclusively on one particular continent. Of course, such critiques are more poignant in the case of Africa, as it bears a long history of international law treating it as barbaric and radically different from the 'civilized West'. The cosmopolitan pretensions of the ICC are thus held against the practice of the ICC, and the argument is made that in this case the Court fits in a longer trend of Western powers using universal values to subdue Africa.

At the same time, the state-based nature of the ICC is recognized, and turned against the Court itself. This type of critique was voiced in relation to the arrest warrant issued against the incumbent president of Sudan, al-Bashir. The arrest warrant followed upon a referral by the Security Council, who referred the situation in Darfur since July 2002 to the ICC via Resolution 1593 (2005). The Office of the Prosecution thereupon decided to go after the president of Sudan and issued two arrest warrants against him. Since the African Union held that the arrest warrant would hamper the fragile peace process in Sudan, it repeatedly asked the Security Council to use its formal powers under article 16 to suspend the arrest warrant. However, the Security Council refused to act upon the requests of the African Union, leaving the latter frustrated and increasingly critical about the functioning of the Council and the ICC. A similar pattern emerged after the ICC issued arrest warrants (this time without prior Security Council referral) against Kenya's president Uhuru Kenyatta and his deputy William Ruto, who were accused of crimes against humanity. The position of the Security Council spurred critiques of neo-imperialism: an exclusive club assumes the power to start investigations into an African president, and subsequently ignores African pleas to take into consideration possible effects on peace and security. Another complicating factor was that Sudan was not a party to the ICC, as were several other African states. What would the situation be if al-Bashir would travel to another non-party state? Would that state be bound by the age-old international rules on state immunity, and thus under an obligation to protect al-Bashir from investigation and arrest? In other words: was the relation between Sudan and other countries one of formal equality, crystalized in the regime of state immunity? Or would that state be bound by the arrest warrant, as this ultimately rooted in the powers of the Security Council, which can create formal inequality between states? Whereas the ICC took the latter position, the African Union held on to the immunity of heads of state. This position was later reconfirmed in relation to the arrest warrants against the Kenyan president and his deputy, and even applied to the newly established African Court of Justice and Human Rights, that is supposed to respect the immunity of African Heads of State and senior officials (Kersten 2014). The struggle between the ICC and the African Union was deepened further when the African Union started to call for (collective) withdrawal from the Statute of the ICC. This call was followed by a number of actual resignations, including the highly symbolic retreat from South Africa.

However, one should be careful to speak of 'the' African critique, as if the whole continent speaks with a single voice. Not all African states share the critique and some states openly criticized (calls for) withdrawal from the Statute. Botswana, for example, argued 'that such a move betrays the rights of the victims of atrocious crimes to justice and also undermines the progress made to date in the global efforts to fight impunity' (Botswana Government Statement, 2016). Within South Africa, high profile figures such as Bishop Tutu characterized calls for withdrawal as 'African leaders (...) effectively seeking a license to kill, maim and oppress their people without consequences' (Tutu 2013). Last but not least, South Africa's constitutional Court decided that withdrawal was invalid and unconstitutional, thus opening up a renewed debate on South Africa's position vis-à-vis the ICC (Democratic Alliance v Minister of International Relations and Cooperation and Others 2017). The 'clash of civilizations' as presented by the African Union is thus not acknowledged by everyone on the African continent. Alongside the narrative of a struggle between a (Western) ICC and a marginalized continent are narratives about Africa's continued commitment to cosmopolitan ideals – even though the actual functioning of the ICC may still be subject to substantive critique.

Conclusion

So far, international law remains an under-researched topic in the literature on Huntington's 'clash of civilizations'. This is remarkable since international law itself was born out of such a clash. For centuries, the relation between Western, self-declared 'civilized' states and other, so-called less civilized parts of the world was one of the core questions in international law. International law was used as a vocabulary to define different levels of civilization and to regulate the relations between these stipulated civilizations. While the language of 'civilization' has now become formally outmoded in international law, many have claimed that regimes such as human rights, trade or security are still based on standards of civilization. Such claims, however, should not be treated as truth claims. More often than not, they are made as part of a normative debate on the nature of international society, and generally they are used to critique existing legal regimes. In this way, such claims actually aim to underscore competing conceptions of international society, based, for example, on notions of formal equality of nations or cosmopolitan equality between cultures and individuals. In this article I have illustrated the mobilization of such competing notions of international society in the African Union's critique of the ICC as a neo-colonial institution. This discussion was also meant to underscore another point: descriptions of the nature of (international) society, such as Huntington's 'clash of civilizations', are also speech acts, yielding presentations of institutional (legal) facts (Ruiter, 1993). In other words: they create imageries of society, which are intrinsically linked to the normative ties that are supposed to exist between its members. International legal argumentation is filled with debates where competing conceptions of society form the basis for normative claims about the relevant agents and their legal relations. The imagery of clashing civilizations is one of them, and one that still holds appeal, as the saga of the African Union's critique of the ICC attests.

References

Aalberts, Tanja and Wouter Werner. 2008. Sovereignty Beyond Borders: Sovereignty, Discipline and Responsibility. In *Sovereignty Games: Instrumentalizing State Sovereignty in Europe and Beyond*, 1st Ed., edited by Rebecca Adler-Nissen and Thomas Gammeltoft-Hansen, 129–149. Palgrave

MacMillan.

Anghie, Antony. 2004. *Imperialism, Sovereingty and the Making of International Law.* Cambridge: Cambridge University Press.

Botswana Government. 2016. Statement on the Withdrawal of South Africa from the Rome Statute of the International Criminal Court. Facebook [web post]. 25 October 2016. https://www.facebook.com/Botswana.Government/posts/1120005841415406 Accessed 21 September 2017.

Craven, Matthew. 2009. *The Decolonization of International Law: State Succession and the Law of Treaties.* Oxford University Press.

Douzinas, Costas. 2007. *Human Rights and Empire: The Political Philosophy of Cosmopolitanism*. Routledge.

Dworkin, Ronald. 1985. *A Matter of Principle*. Cambridge: Harvard University Press.

Gong, Gerrit. 1984. *The Standard of Civilization in International Society.* Oxford University Press.

Huntington, Samuel. 1993. "The Clash of Civilizations?" *Foreign Affairs*, 72(3), pp. 22–49.

Huntington, Samuel. 1997. *The Clash of Civilizations and the Remaking of World Order*. New York: Simon & Schuster.

Kersten, Mark. 2014. "What Gives? African Union Heads of State Immunity." *Africa at LSE* [web blog]. http://blogs.lse.ac.uk/africaatlse/2014/07/14/what-gives-african-union-head-of-state-immunity/Accessed 21 September 2017.

Koskenniemi, Martti. 2002. *The Gentle Civilizer of Nations: The Rise and Fall of International Law 1870–1960*. Cambridge: Cambridge University Press.

Lorimer, James. 2005. *The Institutes of the Law of Nations: A Treatise on the Jural Relations of Separate Political Communities*, Vol. I. Clark, New Jersey: The Lawbook Exchange Limited (originally published in 1883/4 by Blackwood and Sons: Edinburgh).

Miller, Russell A. and Rebecca M. Bratspies, eds. 2008. *Progress in International Law*. Leiden: Matinus Nijhoff.

Nouwen, Sarah and Wouter Werner. 2010. "Doing Justice to the Political: The International Criminal Court in Uganda and Sudan." *European Journal of International Law* 21(4): 941–965.

Rehman, Javaid. 2005. *Islamic State Practices, International Law and the Threat from Terrorism: A Critique of the 'Clash of Civilizations' in the New World Order*. Oxford and Portland: Hart Publishing.

Ruiter, Dick W.P. 1993. *Institutional Legal Facts, Legal Powers and Their Effects*. Springer.

Schmitt, Carl. 2003. *The Nomos of the Earth in the International Law of Jus Publicum Europaeum*. Telos Press (translated by G.L. Ulmen).

Scott, James Brown. 1934. *The Spanish Origins of International Law: Francisco De Vitoria and His Law of Nations*. Oxford: Clarendon Press.

Simpson, Gerry. 2004. *Great Powers and Outlaw States, Unequal Sovereigns in the International Legal Order*. Cambridge: Cambridge University Press.

Tutu, Desmond. 2013. "In Africa Seeking a License to Kill." *New York Times*. http://www.nytimes.com/2013/10/11/opinion/in-africa-seeking-a-license-to-kill.html?mcubz=1 Accessed 21 September 2017.

Wheaton, Henry. 1836. *Elements of International Law. With a Sketch of the History of the Science*. London: Fellowes.

Werner, Wouter. 2016. "What's Going On? Reflections on Kratochwil's Concept of Law." *Millennium: Journal of International Studies* 44(2): 258-268.

Court Cases

Lotus case (France v Turkey). 1927. ser. A no. 10 (Permanent Court of Int'l Justice, P.C.I.J.). http://www.icj-cij.org/files/permanent-court-of-international-justice/serie_A/A_10/30_Lotus_Arret.pdf Accessed 21 September 2017.

Democratic Alliance v Minister of International Relations and Cooperation and Others. 2017. Case No: 83145/2016 (High Court of South Africa (Gauteng Division, Pretoria)). http://saflii.org/za/cases/ZAGPPHC/2017/53.html Accessed 21 September 2017.

12

Dangerous Ties? The (New) 'Clash of Civilizations': Migration and Terrorism

ANA ISABEL XAVIER

New Century, New Clashes?

When the political scientist Samuel P. Huntington first published 'The Clash of Civilizations' (1993), his hypothesis was based on the assumption that future international conflicts would arise from cultural and religious identities. However, the argument that the eight civilizations – Western, Confucian, Japanese, Islamic, Hindu, Slavic-Orthodox, Latin American and possibly African – were morally and politically incompatible, would soon be questioned by scholars all over the world. One of the most famous critics was Edward Said, who replied years later with an essay entitled Clash of Ignorance (2001). This author warned that amplifying an 'us' versus 'them' narrative or a 'west' versus 'Islam' posture is both dangerous and misleading, especially after September 11.

In fact, Huntington believes that 'as people define their identity in ethnic and religious terms, they are likely to see an "us" versus "them" relation existing between themselves and people of different ethnicity or religion' (1993, 29). For the author this would ultimately lead to a confrontation (or even war) between civilizations based on 'who you are' in terms of culture and religion. Moreover, Huntington does not hesitate to claim that Islam has 'bloody borders' (1993, 25), for example with the Orthodox Serbs in the Balkans, the Jews in Israel, the Hindus in India, the Buddhists in Burma or the Catholics in the Philippines.

Despite the numerous 'clashes of scholarships', Huntington's most enduring legacy started to be tested at Europe's borders in the 1990s. Historically envisioned as a reconstruction plan after the Second World War, the origins of the European project were inspired by the ideals of peace, human rights, democracy and good governance, both within and beyond its borders. However, with the end of the Cold War and the humanitarian crisis in the Balkans, the European Economic Community (EEC) was compelled to stand up to new challenges and threats.

To tackle this new strategic environment, the 1992 Maastricht Treaty shaped a new identity – the European Union (EU) – based on a three-pillar structure, including the area of freedom, security and justice. Within these pillars, throughout the years, member states tried to implement the best strategies and policies planned to control and manage its population flows at the national level.

However, the disproportionate burden faced by Greece and Italy in the last couple of years caused a huge tension among EU members. In 2015 alone, more than a million migrants and refugees crossed into Europe. The International Organization for Migration (IOM) estimates that 10,550 migrants and refugees entered Europe by land and 164,779 by sea through 03 December 2017, around 85% arriving first in Italy and Spain and the remainder in Greece and Bulgaria. In addition, 3,086 people were missing or found dead at the Mediterranean by the beginning of December. Moreover, according to the United Nations High Commissioner for Refugees (UNHCR), there were 65.6 million internally displaced persons and 22.5 million refugees worldwide (excluding 5.3 million Palestinians) in 2016. In turn, in the first quarter of 2017, the top three citizenships of asylum seekers in Europe were Syrians (22,500), Afghans (12,500) and Nigerians (11,500 applications). In the same period, according to EUROSTAT, Germany has registered 30% of all applicants in the EU member states, followed by Italy, France, Greece and the United Kingdom.

Bearing all those numbers and facts in mind and considering the absence of a common migration and asylum policy, the EU stance was threefold: political, security and military. The EU tackled this issue through a holistic and comprehensive approach both in the origin, transit and destination countries, blurring the internal and external security nexus (Eriksson and Rhinard 2009; Pastore 2001; Lutterbeck 2001).

Starting with the first dimension (political) we must mention the adoption of the European Agenda on Security (European Commission 2015a), aimed to set out how the Union can bring added value in ensuring security within and beyond its borders. This agenda also acknowledges that member states can no longer succeed fully on their own faced with cross-border terrorism, organized crimes or cybercrime which require indeed an effective and coordinated response at the European level. Following this document, also in 2015, the European Commission presented the European Agenda on Migration (2015b) that set both short (prevent further losses of migrants' lives at sea) and medium/long term priorities (reducing the incentives for irregular migration; saving lives and securing the external borders; strengthening the common asylum policy; and developing a new policy on legal migration) to better manage the EU's external borders along with its member states.

In terms of security (the second dimension), three facts are worth mentioning. First, the EU-Turkey agreement (March 2016) aiming to restrain the influx of people crossing to Greek islands and to assure that for every Syrian migrant sent back to Turkey, one Syrian already in Turkey will be resettled in the EU. This deal has been strongly criticized because, in return, Turkey might be encouraged to push more political concessions in the future (Hakura 2016) and the EU has apparently resigned on its responsibilities to provide protection and security to those in need (Collett 2016).

Second is the strengthening of the EU's cooperation with Western Balkan countries – the frontline of the Eastern route – by providing them with technical, humanitarian and financial assistance. In fact, on 26 October 2015, a meeting between the leaders of Albania, Bulgaria, Croatia, FYR Macedonia, Germany, Greece, Hungary, Romania, Serbia and Slovenia agreed on an action plan with the aim of avoiding a possible humanitarian crisis along the transit route. This regional approach also relies on strong coordination and consultation with Turkey as, by land or sea, thousands of migrants have entered Bulgaria or Greece with the aim of reaching the Schengen area.

The third fact also relates to the political dimension and is the implementation of a European Border and Coast Guard to protect and enhance the security and management of the EU's External Borders. This initiative was announced by President Juncker in his State of the Union Speech on 9 September 2015 as part of a comprehensive approach set out by the European Agenda on Migration. The implementation of a European Border and Coast Guard expands the mandate of Frontex (the European Agency for the Management of Operational Cooperation at the External Borders of the EU) in the fields of external border management. In addition, the EU's rebranding of the latter as the European Border and Coast Guard Agency was meant to give more visibility to its new tasks. In this regard, on 25 January 2017, a new package of four documents on migration and security was approved by the European Commission (European Commission 2017a; 2017b; 2017c; 2017d).

The last dimension is the military. Indeed, another key pillar of the EU institutional approach to cope with the migration and refugee crisis is exemplified by the ability to deploy missions and operations to identify, capture and destroy vessels used by smugglers framed by the Common Security and Defense Policy (CSDP). Thus, following a tragic Libyan migrant shipwreck in April 2015, the EU launched a military operation – European Union Naval Force Mediterranean (EUNAVFOR Med) – with the aim of countering established refugee smuggling routes in the Mediterranean. This was agreed on 18 May 2015 as a three-phase military operation in accordance with the procedures of international law (Tardy 2015): the first phase would focus on the surveillance and assessment of human smuggling and trafficking networks in the Southern Central Mediterranean; the second and third phases aimed to search, seize and disrupt the assets of smugglers, though it depends on the partnership with Libyan authorities upon a United Nations Security Council resolution. This mission counterparts Operation Triton as a border security operation conducted by Frontex, under Italian command, that began on 1 November 2014 and involved voluntary contributions from Croatia, Iceland, Finland, Norway, Sweden, Germany, the Netherlands, France, Spain, Ireland, Portugal, Austria, Switzerland, Romania, Poland, Lithuania and Malta.

In October 2015, the Council renamed this mission to EUNAVFOR MED Operation Sophia, honoring the rescue of a baby girl born on a vessel on 22 August off the coast of Libya. On 20 June 2016, the Council of the European Union decided to extend Sophia's mandate until the end of July 2017 by adding the training of the Libyan Coastguard and Navy and contributing to the implementation of the UN arms embargo on the high seas off the coast of Libya as supporting tasks. On 25 July 2017, the Council extended once again the EUNAVFOR MED Operation Sophia up until 31 December 2018 and amended the mandate in order to set up a monitoring mechanism of trainees to ensure the long-term efficiency of the training of the Libyan Coastguard, conduct new surveillance activities and gather information on illegal trafficking of oil exports from Libya in accordance with UNSCR 2146 (2014) and 2362 (2017), and enhance the possibilities for sharing information on human trafficking with member states' law enforcement agencies, FRONTEX and EUROPOL.

Europe's Dilemmas: A Social Constructivist Approach

With the disintegration of the bipolar confrontation of the Cold War and the start of globalization, International Relations research and teaching patterns in the last two decades of the twentieth century shifted to a new 'reflectivist critique of the scientific approach to the study of social sciences' (Behravesh

2011). As a result, the assumption that the fundamental structures of international politics are not only shaped by a neorealist anarchist power politics, but also by ongoing processes of social practice, paved the way for constructivists (Adler 2001; Onuf 1998; Wendt 1992; Zehfuss 2002) to challenge the nature of interactions and, thus, identity. In fact, social constructivist authors tend to acknowledge that 'the structures of human association are determined primarily by shared ideas rather than material forces, and that the identities and interests of purposive actors are constructed by these shared ideas rather than given by nature (Wendt 1999, 1). Moreover, one of the key features of International Relations constructivist approaches is the role that social norms play in states' identities.

This assumption is theoretically useful to help us to explore four practical dilemmas, questions or clashes: (1) the perceptions by EU citizens on the balance between freedom and security; (2) the rise of Far-Right movements and the growth of Islamism and terrorist attacks in Europe; (3) the migration flows in an ageing Europe in need of a more qualified manpower; and (4) the challenges of integration, counter radicalization and deradicalization.

In what concerns the first 'clash' – the perceptions by EU citizens on the balance between freedom and security – the results of the Eurobarometer Standard surveys (Autumn 2015 and Spring 2016) illustrate that Europeans see immigration (48% in 2016, down ten percent from 2015) and terrorism (39%, up 14% from 2015) as the major challenges the EU is facing. Furthermore, 67% of Europeans are in favor of a common European migration policy and 58% have a positive opinion on the migration of people from other EU member states. Moreover, 79% of Europeans are in favor of the free movement of EU citizens who can live, work, study and do business anywhere in the EU. However, almost 60% also have a negative opinion on the immigration of people from outside the EU. In addition, the data also reveals terrorism as a source of growing concern following the terrorist attacks in France (7 January and 13 November 2015 in Paris, 14 July 2016 in Nice), Belgium (22 March 2016) and Germany (July and December 2016).

As a result, two misconceptions emerged: first, that there are no differences between economic migrants and refugees, which is contentious, as asylum seekers are entitled to humanitarian protection and specific rights covered by the United Nations 1951 Geneva Convention, while economic migrants are subject to national laws; second, that these new migratory movements are spreading Islamism in Europe.

This leads to the second 'clash', which is the rise of Far-Right movements and the growth of Islamism and terrorist attacks in Europe. This 'clash' is being politically exposed by some extremist right-wing populist parties and movements (Greven 2016) that helped to foster hostile feelings towards immigrants and refugees. We are referring to political parties such as National Front (France), UKIP (UK), Lega Nord (Italy), Golden Dawn (Greece), Freedom Party (Holland), Jobbik Swedish Democrats (Sweden), Progress Party (Norway), Finns (Finland), Danish People's Party (Denmark), Freedom Party (Austria), Swiss People's Party (Switzerland) and Alternative für Deutschland (Germany), that claim that a series of terrorist incidents were caused by refugees or asylum seekers. For example, between 18 and 24 July 2016, a series of attacks took place in Germany (the EU member state with the highest number of asylum applications) involving an Afghan refugee that injured five people in a train (18th), an Iranian refugee that killed nine people in Munich (22nd), a Syrian refugee that killed a woman in Reutlingen (24th) and in Ansbach, a suicide attack of a Syrian refugee (24th). Also, the attack on the Breitscheid Square in Berlin on 19 December 2016 was allegedly headed by Anis Amri, a Tunisian who had seen his asylum application denied and was using 14 different identities to access social benefits and trick the intelligence services. Recent studies (TESAT 2017, 22–25) confirm that DAESH has indeed been, and possibly continues to be, exploiting refugees and migrants' routes to send individuals to Europe to commit acts of terrorism.

Therefore, it is not surprising that some countries have been building walls to control borders and prevent radical Jihadists or other members of terrorist cells from succeeding in reaching Western Europe from the Balkans or Mediterranean route. In this regard, it was widely covered by the European media the impact of the 32km wall between Bulgaria and Turkey, the Evros wall between Greece and Turkey of 12.5km, or the 175km border between Hungary and Serbia.

However, while a Pew Research study estimates that by 2030 Muslims will represent eight per cent of Europe's total population and will reach ten per cent by 2050, exceeding Christians worldwide by 2070 (Yuhas 2015), some authors (Bullard 2016) argue that the youngest generation seems to be disengaged of any religious belief.

Moreover, an ageing Europe needs to attract young people, or it will face major problems in terms of social welfare systems, losing geopolitical competitiveness (ESPAS 2012). This represents the third 'clash' (the migration flows in an ageing Europe in need of a more qualified and sustainable labor force). In fact, according to the Eurostat statistics, the share of the population aged 65 years and over increased 2.4 percentage points between 2006 and 2016 for the EU28, while the share of the population aged less than 15 years in the EU28 population decreased by 0.4 percentage points.

To conclude, the fourth 'clash' concerns the challenges of integration, counter radicalization and deradicalization. Among the 28 member states, the question of cultural and religious identity (the core focus of Huntington's piece) is being tackled in two different ways (Aleksynska and Algan 2010): either through an assimilation (when a minority communities' identity is absorbed by the dominant features of the majority culture), or through an integration perspective (the minority culture is harmoniously accommodated into an intercultural society where all get access to the same opportunities, rights and duties). Although the European Institutions have been striving for an overall integration policy (Berlinghoff 2014; Entzinger and Biezeveld 2003), rising criminality and terrorism along with unprecedented migratory pressure from the Mediterranean and Balkans routes have encouraged more protectionist, isolationist and sovereign approaches all over European states (Lacroix 2015; Malik 2015; Zappi 2003).

What is rather interesting is that, in his book, Huntington lists five factors that have exacerbated the conflictual nature of Islam and Christianity (1996, 211), and one of the factors relates to the fact that Muslim population growth has generated large numbers of unemployed and dissatisfied youth that become recruits to Islamic causes. Should we then accept that a given economic, social and cultural profile might lead to radicalization and terrorism?

Huntington argued that 'for the relevant future, there will be no universal civilization, but instead a world of different civilizations, each of which will have to learn to coexist with the others' (1993, 49). For sure, the main way to address this problem does not lie only in the generic, targeted and indicated prevention measures (European Commission 2017, 20–35) aimed at the integration of the communities of immigrants and refugees, but also in deradicalization (any measures or programs aimed to reintegrate those already radicalized into society or at least dissuade them from extreme and violent religious or political ideologies) and counter radicalization (any preventative effort aimed at preventing radicalization from taking place). In this regard, it is worth mentioning Schmid's (2013) effort in listing several national and local lessons learned, as well as the Council of the European Union initiative to draft revised Guidelines for the EU Strategy for Combating Radicalization and Recruitment to Terrorism (2017). In addition, EU institutions and national governments must be able to deliver and strike a balance between freedom, justice and security, as well as a sustainable welfare state, to fully accommodate all the cultural identities in European member states no matter its nationality or religion.

Conclusion

Twenty-five years after Huntington's article was published, Europe is struggling with migration and terrorism, which are a top priority for EU citizens and governments. We cannot figure out what would be Huntington's perspective on today's challenges and threats, but as far as this essay is concerned, I believe that the author never meant to encourage a 'clash of civilizations' ('west against the rest'). Instead, Huntington meant to warn that cultural identities, antagonisms and affiliations will play a major role in relations between states and that the shape of interactions between cultural identities might be the latest phase in the evolution of conflict in the modern world.

Throughout this chapter, I have identified the three dimensions of the EU's institutional approach to this issue (political, security and military) concluding that a new 'border's diplomacy' (Parkes 2016) that addresses the root causes of underdevelopment and conflict, protecting people in need and providing integration through solidarity and mutual awareness is needed. In fact, we assumed that prevention, cooperation and multilateralism are the three key features that can be enhanced to depoliticize, desecuritize and demilitarize the ties between civilization, migration, terrorism and thus, avoid cultural and identity clashes with unpredictable consequences for humankind. For that purpose, the political, security and military measures taken by the European Union since 2015, and that we have mentioned throughout this essay, are interesting to follow in the future as most of their practical implications are still far from being accomplished.

In fact, there is still room for improvement as recognized by the European Commission when launching the European Agenda on Migration in May 2015, namely in what concerns the cooperation with third countries of origin (Syria, Libya, Iraq, the Sahel region, Afghanistan and Yemen) and transit (Egypt, Tunisia, Algeria, Niger and Mali) within a regional comprehensive approach. Also, the existing bilateral and regional cooperation platforms (Rabat Process, Khartoum Process, the Budapest Process, the EU-Africa Migration and Mobility Dialogue) must be accurately promoted as they represent an important forum for migration and security dialogue. The EU Delegations and UN special representatives in key countries (Egypt, Algeria, Morocco, Tunisia, Niger, Senegal, Sudan, Turkey, Pakistan, Lebanon and Jordan) must work closely with Immigration Liaison Officers Network, local authorities and community leaders. Border control in North Africa and the Horn of Africa must be enhanced through the implementation of local support centers in coordination with the IOM, the UNHCR and the local authorities. In the destination countries, integration policies must be fostered and deradicalization (as well as counter radicalization) must be developed in cooperation with intelligence services and community religious leaders. Legal and highly qualified migration should be encouraged (a blue card and a fast track procedure is on the way), and a global commons solidarity regime must be negotiated within the framework of the United Nations. This roadmap set in 2015 by the European Commission, following the presentation of the European Agenda on Migration, is still in need of a fruitful implementation.

To conclude, at least one question remains: 25 years after Huntington's article, are we facing or moving to a new 'clash of civilizations'? What seems certain is that dangerous ties are being nourished every day in the European society while we witness the growth of populist movements against refugees and migrants claiming a connection between Islam and terrorism.

References

Adler, Emmanuel. 2001. "Constructivism and International Relations." In *Handbook of International Relations*, edited by W. Carlsnaes, T. Risse and B. A. Simmons, 95–118. London: SAGE Publications.

Aleksynska, Mariya and Yann Algan. 2010. "Assimilation and Integration of Immigrants in Europe." Discussion Paper No. 5185. *Forschungsinstitut zur Zukunft der Arbeit Institute for the Study of Labor*. http://ftp.iza.org/dp5185.pdf Accessed 12 September 2017.

Berlinghoff, Marcel. 2014. "Migration and Cultural Integration in Europe." *Conference Report Brussels*, 11 December 2013. IfA (Institut für Auslandsbeziehungen), Stuttgart and Berlin. http://www.ifa.de/fileadmin/pdf/edition/berlinghoff_migration_integration_europe.pdf Accessed 10 October 2017.

Bullard, Gabe. 2016. "The World's Newest Major Religion: No Religion." *National Geographic*. http://news.nationalgeographic.com/2016/04/160422-atheism-agnostic-secular-nones-rising-religion/ Accessed 15 September 2017.

Collett, Elizabeth. 2016. "The Paradox of the EU-Turkey Refugee Deal." *Migration Policy Institute*. http://www.migrationpolicy.org/news/paradox-eu-turkey-refugee-deal Accessed 19 September 2017.

Council of the European Union. 2017. "Draft Revised Guidelines for the EU Strategy for Combating Radicalisation and Recruitment to Terrorism" (9646/17). *Council of the European Union*.

Entzinger, Han and Renske Biezeveld. 2003. "Benchmarking in Immigrant Integration." *European Research Centre on Migration and Ethnic Relations*. https://ec.europa.eu/home-affairs/sites/homeaffairs/files/e-library/documents/policies/legal-migration/pdf/general/benchmarking_final_en.pdf Accessed 10 October 2017.

Eriksson, Johan and Mark Rhinard. 2009. "The Internal-External Security Nexus – Notes on an Emerging Research Agenda." *Cooperation and conflict: Journal of Nordic International Studies Association* 44(3): 243–267.

European Strategy and Policy Analysis System. 2012. "Global Trends 2030: Citizens in an Interconnected and Polycentric World." *European Union Institute for Security Studies*.

European Commission. 2015a. "The European Agenda on Security." *Communication from the Commission to the European Parliament, the Council, the European Economic and Social Committee and the Committee of the Regions*. Strasbourg, 28 April.

European Commission. 2015b. "A European Agenda on Migration." *Communication from the Commission to the European Parliament, the Council, the European Economic and Social Committee and the Committee of the Regions*. Brussels, 13 May.

European Commission. 2017. "The Contribution of Youth Work to Preventing Marginalisation and Radicalisation." *Results of the expert group set up under the European Union Work Plan for Youth for 2016–2018*.

European Commission. 2017a. "Migration on the Central Mediterranean Route: Managing Flows, Saving Lives." *Joint Communication to the European Parliament, the European Council and the Council*. Brussels, 25 January.

European Commission. 2017b. "Proposal for a Council Implementing Decision Setting out a Recommendation for Prolonging Temporary Internal Border Control in Exceptional Circumstances Putting the Overall Functioning of the Schengen Area at Risk." Brussels, 25 January.

European Commission. 2017c. "Report from the Commission to the European Parliament, the European Council and the Council on the Operationalization of the European Border and Coast Guard." Brussels, 06 September.

European Commission. 2017d. "Communication from the Commission to the European Parliament, the European Council and the Council, Fourth Progress Report Towards an Effective and Genuine Security Union." Strasbourg, 16 May.

Greven, Thomas. 2016. "The Rise of Right-wing Populism in Europe and the United States: A Comparative Perspective." *Friedrich Ebert Stiftung*.

Hakura, Fadi. 2016. "The EU-Turkey Refugee Deal Solves Little." https://www.chathamhouse.org/publications/twt/eu-turkey-refugee-deal-solves-little Accessed 10 September 2017.

Huntington, Samuel P. 1993. "The Clash of Civilizations?" *Foreign Affairs* 72, no. 3 (Summer): 22–49

Huntington, Samuel P. 1996. *The Clash of Civilizations and the Remaking of World Order*. New York: Simon and Schuster.

Lacroix, Thomas. 2015. "The Long, Troubled History of Assimilation in France." *The Conversation*. http://theconversation.com/the-long-troubled-history-of-assimilation-in-france-51530 Accessed 20 September 2017.

Lutterbeck, Derek. 2007. "Blurring the Dividing Line: the Convergence of Internal and External Security in Western Europe." *European Security* 14(2): 231–253.

Malik, Kenan. 2015. "Terrorism Has Come About in Assimilationist France and also in Multicultural Britain. Why Is That?" *The Guardian*. https://www.theguardian.com/commentisfree/2015/nov/15/multiculturalism-assimilation-britain-france Accessed 10 September 2017.

Onuf, Nicholas. 1998. "Constructivism: A User's Manual." In *International Relations in a Constructed World*, edited by Vendulka Kubálková, Nicholas Onuf, Paul Kowert, 58–78. Milton Park: Routledge.

Parkes, Roderick. 2016. "The Internal-External Nexus: Re-Bordering Europe." *European Union Institute for Security Studies*. http://www.iss.europa.eu/uploads/media/Brief_28_Borders.pdf Accessed 10 September 2017.

Pastore, Ferruccio. 2001. "Reconciling the Prince's Two 'Arms': Internal-External Security Policy Coordination." In *Occasional papers 30, Institute for Security Studies*, October. http://www.iss.europa.eu/uploads/media/occ030.pdf Accessed 10 September 2017

Said, Edward W. 2001. "The Clash of Ignorance." *The Nation*. https://www.thenation.com/article/clash-ignorance/ Accessed 10 September 2017.

Schmid, Alex P. 2013. "Radicalisation, De-Radicalisation, Counter-Radicalisation: A Conceptual Discussion and Literature Review." *ICCT Research Paper*, March. https://www.icct.nl/download/file/ICCT-Schmid-Radicalisation-De-Radicalisation-Counter-Radicalisation-March-2013.pdf Accessed 10 September 2017.

Tardy, Thierry. 2015. "Operation Sophia Tackling the refugee crisis with military means." *European Union Institute for Security Studies*. Brief Issue 30, September. http://www.iss.europa.eu/uploads/media/Brief_30_Operation_Sophia.pdf Accessed 10 October 2017.

TESAT. 2017. "European Union Situation and Trend Report." *European Union Agency for Law Enforcement Cooperation*.

Wendt, Alexander. 1992. "Anarchy is What States Make of It: the Social Construction of Power Politics." *International Organization* 46(2): 391–425.

Wendt, Alexander. 1999. "Social Theory of International Politics." Cambridge: Cambridge University Press.

Yuhas, Alan. 2015. "Muslim Population in Europe to Reach 10% by 2050, New Forecast Shows." *The Guardian*. https://www.theguardian.com/world/2015/apr/02/muslim-population-growth-christians-religion-pew Accessed 12 November 2017.

Zappi, Sylvia. 2003. "French Government Revives Assimilation Policy." *Migration Policy Institute*. https://www.migrationpolicy.org/article/french-government-revives-assimilation-policy Accessed 10 September 2017.

Zehfuss, Maja. 2002. *Constructivism in International Relations*. Cambridge, UK: Cambridge University Press.

13

An Alternative for Germany? Tracing Huntington's 'Clash of Civilizations' Thesis in a Right-Wing Populist Party

JAN LÜDERT

Founded in 2013 as a protest party, the Alternative for Germany (AfD) gained representation in fourteen federal state parliaments and, since September 2017, holds 92 seats in the Bundestag, Germany's federal parliament. Similar to other European right-wing parties, like the Netherlands' Party for Freedom or France's National Front, the AfD has rapidly morphed into a populist party with a strong anti-Islam agenda and rhetoric. This chapter traces Samuel Huntington's civilization thesis of future conflict in the AfD's party program 'Islam is not a part of Germany'. The author argues that the party's fixed conception of Islam parallels Huntington's conceptualization of civilizations and fault line conflicts. By making this argument, the author explores whether and how AfD party members draw on Huntington's civilizational hypothesis in a broader attempt to entrench a German nationalist and anti-Islam agenda. Second, this chapter focuses on AfD proposals to ban minarets and burqas. These policy prescriptions are read against criticisms of the party's intrinsic 'clash of civilizations' logic by mainstream party members, leading German Islamic leaders, and other public actors. Third, the chapter ties these developments into a discussion of how the federal government's response to the Syrian refugee crisis offered AfD party members opportunities to gain political advantage by establishing an anti-Islam agenda – an agenda that is rooted in a 'clash of civilizations' thesis of perceived fault line conflicts and a deep-seated desire for cultural homogeneity. Finally, building on the above, this chapter briefly assesses the Alternative for Germany's prospects since entering the Bundestag in the fall of 2017.

The late Samuel Huntington put forth his 'Clash of Civilizations' (CoC) thesis in which he envisioned that the future of global politics would be based on inter-civilizational and cultural conflict; conflict that, in particular, would take place between the Islamic world and the West. The twenty-first century, accordingly, would no longer be a battleground between economic, ideological or political struggles. While many of Huntington's arguments are incontrovertible, his most contentious claim was that the fault lines of future discord would originate from the Islamic world, a civilization he asserts to be intrinsically violent and incorrigibly illiberal (Huntington, 1993, 21–49). On the surface, events such as 9/11, recent terrorist attacks around Europe and elsewhere, and the rise of ISIS all seem to validate his thesis.

Notwithstanding, scholars have criticized his overbroad conceptualizations of civilization and culture. These scholars contest his thesis because it lacks convincing empirical evidence (Russett, O'neal, and Cox 2000; Henderson and Tucker 2001; Chiozza 2002). A main line of contention against the CoC thesis is that it offers an impoverished and oversimplified view of pluralist cultures (Katzenstein 2009). Huntington, these scholars counter, assumes that civilizations are monolithic and homogenous and that there exists an unchanging duality between us and them. The religion of Islam, these authors go on to argue, is 'fabricated to whip up feelings of hostility and antipathy' in the West (Said 2001, 9). I agree that a Huntingtonian worldview risks conflating violent extremisms with Islam itself. It ultimately offers insufficient leverage for understanding a complex world.

Despite its serious conceptual flaws and wanting empirical support, ideas espoused in the CoC thesis continue to resonate today. The focus of this chapter is to invite scholarly focus on how populist European figures and parties draw on an overbroad and fatalistic CoC logic. These actors, like Huntington, foresee the end of the West through a hostile takeover by radical Islam and, they would add, Muslim immigration to the West. This chapter traces these developments in light of the rapid ascent of the Alternative for Germany (AfD) on the German political scene. It focuses on the parallels between Samuel Huntington's civilizations thesis of conflict and the ideological framework of the AfD party's platform which overtly makes the claim that 'Islam is not a part of Germany'.

The Alternative for Germany: A Brief History

Following its establishment in the spring of 2013, the Alternative for Germany experienced an unprecedented ascent as a political party (Niedermayer 2015). The party originated against the backdrop of Greece's sovereign debt bailout and the pursuant Euro crisis. The AfD was at first perceived to be a party of academics – not least because an economist, Bernd Lucke, founded it. Although failing to secure a seat in the Bundestag by a small margin in 2014, the party secured seven seats in the European Parliament, and representation in 14 state parliaments between 2014 and 2016 (Bundeszentrale für politische Bildung, 2107). In Saxony-Anhalt and Mecklenburg-Western Pomerania, 24.2% and 20.8% of voters respectively cast their vote for the AfD. In other state elections, some five to fifteen percent of the electorate voted for the AfD. Most recently, in Germany's federal elections, held in late September 2017, the party received 12.6% of votes and as such is now the Bundestag's third largest fraction. Recent studies have revealed that the party was able to take votes from all of Germany's established mainstream parties, and it currently boasts more than 23,000 members. No other newly-formed party in German post-war politics has ever had as much electoral success.

With Lucke's departure following intense factional infighting in 2015, the AfD began to fixate less on the Euro crisis and reoriented its stance to offer voters a far-right nativist home. The one issue that brings AfD voters together is an intense concern over immigration and Islam. With such populist appeal, the AfD was predicted to join the Bundestag in September 2017. Surveys by INFRATEST DIMAP, a polling organization, show that the AfD's voter demographic fit a certain typology. Supporters are predominantly male, between the ages of 25 and 44. Voters over the age of 60 are less represented but are nevertheless present in the ranks of AfD supporters. INFRATEST DIMAP also showed that the AfD syphoned votes from all established parties and draws support from across all social classes. About a third of its supporters are laborers and another third are unemployed. Voter demographics illustrate that its base predominantly completed *Realschule* – a typical degree outcome for most Germans that does not qualify for entering universities.

AfD's appeal among voters and its political gains have not been the result of a sophisticated agenda and platform. Its success is a result of offering an outlet for disgruntled voters ('Wutbürger') for whom the AfD framed an anti-establishment and outsider identity. The party articulated a political home for these voters under the slogan 'a credo for truth' (Mut zur Wahrheit) which it focuses against the 'elite political caste', the 'lying' media and all those who use 'thought control' in the name of political correctness, which, the party contends, discourages public discourse on entire themes that are on the minds of German people (AfD 2016). The Syrian refugee crisis provided the AfD with a boost. This was particularly observable after chancellor Merkel's open-door policy of welcoming nearly a million refugees took effect in 2015.

The AfD has, following stark divisions within its leadership, taken a sharp right-wing populist and national-conservative turn based on a strong anti-Islam agenda. This move began when the far-right patriotic faction called for a tough stance against the 'Islamization of the occident' (Islamisierung des Abendlandes) by connecting it to a call 'against the delusion of a multicultural society' (Patriotische Platform 2014). The AfD, as such, co-evolved as a political ally of the protest movement 'Patriotic Europeans Against the Islamization of the West' (Patriotische Europäer gegen die Islamisierung des Abendlandes, PEGIDA) (Grabow 2016). Under an umbrella of fighting a culture war ('Kulturkampf'), both forces have since mid-2015 mobilized a broad spectrum of Germans through their shared intent to fend off foreign infiltration, foremost by Muslim immigrants and refugees.

A basic fear the AfD and PEGIDA see on the horizon is what they have coined 'ethnic redeployment' ('Umvolkung'). By allowing for unchecked immigration, the Islamization of German society will lead to a consequential loss of German culture and identity and ultimately to a breakdown of state and society itself. The AfD centers this doomsday argument on what it views as the entrenchment of parallel Islamic societies within Germany – including the notion that Sharia will, one day, supplant the rule of law (Patzelt 2016). Frauke Petry, a former party leader, went as far as to call upon Germans to reclaim the word 'Volk' from its national-socialist connotations and to reassert a bottled-up patriotism instead (BBC 2016). Such pronouncements are not isolated. Bernd Höcke, a member of the far-right faction, repeatedly invokes the 'Fatherland' and 'Volk'. He stresses that Germany must overcome its collective national guilt and make a '180 degree' turn to regain its national pride (Taub and Fisher 2017). The AfD's portrayal of Germany's national identity as being undermined by migration and multiculturalism dovetails with one of Huntington's predictions: 'civilization rallying' by 'populist politicians, religious leaders and the media' will arouse 'mass support' and will be used to pressure governments (Huntington 1993, 38). The remainder of the chapter traces these and other overlapping CoC declarations through an analysis of the AfD's party program 'Islam is not a part of Germany'.

The AfD Fills the Gap between Reality and Perception

According to statistics, some 4.5 million Muslims reside in Germany. Given Germany's population of 82.2 million, this means that approximately 5.5% of its people have a religious background in Islam. A vast majority of the Muslim community in Germany are of Turkish origin and descent, first arriving as so-called guest workers (Gastarbeiter) in the 1960s, with a second group fleeing from war-torn regions in Afghanistan, Iraq and Syria. Almost one in four, or some 1.2 million Muslims, moved to Germany fairly recently and predominantly due to the Syrian refugee crisis (Stichs 2016). These statistics stand in stark contrast to perception, however. According to a recent IPSOS poll, Germans grossly overestimate the current number and projected growth of Muslims in Germany. The poll revealed that Germans think that some 21% of its population is Muslim (IPSOS 2016). This four-fold gap between reality and perception is bridged by the AfD with an anti-Islam agenda for a disgruntled and susceptible electorate.

In late April 2016, the AfD adopted a new party program for the 2017 federal elections which insists that 'Islam is not part of Germany'. Stating further that the 'spread of Islam' poses a 'great danger for our nation, our society and our values'. The party manifesto argued that Islamic states seek to broaden their own power bases by building and staffing mosques on German territory. These states, the AfD explains, are engaged in a cultural war and perpetuate a form of religious imperialism. A trend which has to be halted (AfD 2017, 34–35). The central political goal for the party is 'self-preservation, not self-destruction of our state and people' (AfD 2017, 28). To this end, the party proposes a tightening of border controls to avert the 'massive influx' of people and especially those from African and predominantly Muslim states: regions, the party alleges, that do not belong to the 'West and its values' (AfD 2017, 18).

Culture as a Great Divider

The cadence of these arguments bears a striking resemblance to realist assumptions of state survival, anarchy, and the inevitability of conflict. The AfD justify them as political prudence and draw upon Samuel Huntington's argument concerning the great divisions among humankind and the hypothesis that cultural blocs will become the primary source of future conflict. It is evident that a 'growth of civilization-consciousness' – or the 'trends toward a turning inward' – as espoused by Huntington shows up in the AfD's nationalist and nativist agenda (Huntington 1993, 26). Certainly, the AfD mobilizes its support via a Huntingtonian prescription of rallying around common religious and civilizational signifiers. For the AfD, a 'clash of civilizations' is imminent.

At the domestic, or micro-level, 'adjacent groups along the fault lines between civilizations struggle, often violently, over the control of territory and each other' (Huntington 1993, 29). Orthodox Islam, as the AfD echoes, makes a claim to power ('Herrschaftsanspruch') and is in militant opposition to all 'infidels'; read: the people of Europe and of the West. Huntington's micro-level conflict, the party agrees, is already common-place in German cities where 'Islamic parallel societies with Sharia judges' rule entire communities outside the rule of German law. Immigrants, in order to have a right to stay in Germany, the party demands, owe allegiance to German values ('Bringschuld') and must assimilate to its leading culture ('Leitkultur') (AfD 2017, 32). Integration, for the AfD, 'does not mean that Germany adjusts to Muslims. Integration, means that Muslims assimilate to Germany' (Afd 2017, 45). Huntington uses religion as the basic element of culture – apart from kin, language, values – to build a spurious and circular causal relationship in which religion is the cultural glue of civilizations. Just as the AfD, he describes the decline of the West and invokes a sense of urgency because immigration threatens Western civilization.

By seeking to bolster a cultural core in which Germany is seen to be the center of the West, the AfD equally claims to draw upon the values of 'Christianity, antiquity, and principles of humanism and the enlightenment', 'the liberal rule of law, our appreciation for educations, the arts and sciences as well as social market capitalism as an expression of human creativity'. With this basis, the AfD's central goal is to 'protect' German culture from Muslim infiltration as well as the ideology of multiculturalism. Both of these, the party manifesto alleges, inevitably lead to 'domestic conflict and the dismemberment of the state' (AfD 2017, 47). AfD pronouncements are close to verbatim to Huntington's take on 'Western ideas of individualism, liberalism, constitutionalism, human rights, equality, liberty, the rule of law, democracy, free markets, the separation of church and state', and as the AfD's view highlights, 'often have little resonance in Islamic, Confucian, Japanese, Hindu, Buddhist or Orthodox cultures' (Huntington 1993, 40).

Undoubtedly, Huntington's 'descriptive hypotheses' and his 'implications for Western policy' to mitigate against the CoC show up in AfD's policy statements:

> The culture war between the West and Islam, which is already taking place in Europe, as a doctrine of salvation and the bearers of non-assimilative cultural traditions and rights, can only be averted by a series of defensive and restrictive measures which prevent a further destruction of European values [and] of the coexistence of enlightened citizens. The AfD will not allow Germany to lose its cultural face from misunderstood tolerance (AfD 2017, 47).

Micro-level and fault line conflicts perpetuated by illiberal Islam, as the AfD declares, are reality. They are a serious German domestic and European problem. They not only exist in Islam abroad but are more immediately dangerous because of their existence within states, the EU, the liberal West, and Christian civilization more broadly. As AfD party vice chairman Alexander Gauland put it, 'Islam' is problematic insofar as 'Muslim believers are not a problem, but Islam as a religion is' (Tagesschau 2017). Beatrix von Storch, an AfD representative to the European parliament, explains it this way: 'The biggest threat to democracy and freedom today stems from political Islam' (Handelsblatt 2017).

These understandings by leading AfD figures are worth noting because criticisms of the CoC equally apply to the AfD. Both use a reductive argument that essentializes Islam and especially as a religion with a propensity for conflict while equally ignoring Muslims' multifaceted identities, religious affiliations, and pluralistic cultures. Just as they view the West as a coherent and homogenous cultural bloc, so they disregard complexity in favor of broad-brush demarcations between the West and the rest. What permeates through the AfD's party program is a Huntingtonian worldview: a reified Islam, understood as a retrograde, barbarian and savage 'other', threatening the survival of a progressive and peaceful West that is retrenching and under attack. In the same vein as Huntington constructs his argument, the AfD also perceives a double threat: the West is in decline while Islam is a force introducing conflict. The AfD therefore also needs to be understood as a party that holds onto a nativist ideology within this civilization-based logic. The AfD harbors a deep-seated desire for a homogenous German core and 'leading culture', a culture that non-natives – by their presence, ideas and way of life – fundamentally undermine and threaten. As Huntington would have it, a world of clashing civilizations 'is inevitably a world of double standards: people apply one standard to their kin-countries and a different standard to others' (Huntington 1993, 36).

The AfD opposes criticism which claims that the party is Islamophobic, xenophobic or racist, asserting instead that it is engaged in a rational discourse of critiquing religion (AfD 2017, 34). The AfD's platform presents the following critiques of Islamic culture: the minaret is a symbol of dominance which institutes religious imperialism; Burqas and Niqabs should be banned from public because they do not conform with the principles of equality; and that the financing of mosques by foreign governments constitutes territorial encroachment on German territory – a practice that should be outlawed (AfD 2017a). These calls – apart from being difficult to reconcile with the German constitution, which guarantees religious freedom and expression – are at odds with the party's own commitment to the rule of law. Formulations chosen in the party program tread a fine line of constitutional conformity; party leaders and supporters are less nuanced. Jörg Meuthen, a party spokesman, is steadfast: conflict is inherent to Islam but not to other religions. He mused that although only a few Muslims are terrorists, almost all of recent terrorism has roots in Islam. More to the point, Albrecht

Glaser, a member of the AfD's leadership circle, stated that Islam is a construction that does not know religious freedom and does not respect it, and where it reigns, stifles every kind of freedom of religion. One who treats the constitution in such a way forfeits their rights under the constitution (Leif, 2017).

Unsurprisingly, such views invite criticism from all of the established German parties, religious leaders, and the media alike. For example, the Social Democratic Party (SPD) called the AfD's criticism of Islam an attempt to put an entire religion under general suspicion, to be not in conformity with the constitution, and to draw on unsubstantiated facts to make its case (SPD 2017). Die Linke countered, stating that to define an entire religion as conflictual is 'just as absurd' as to argue that Christianity and the Ku Klux Klan are one and the same (Die Linke 2017). Green party leadership member Katrin Göring-Eckhard noted that the AfD's reactionary political line would soon be uncovered as baseless in its assessment and ineffectual in its proposals. Religious leaders are equally united against the AfD. Aiman Mazyek, the head of Germany's Muslim Council, warned that the AfD is a divisive force without solutions to real problems. Heinrich Bedford-Strohm, head of the Protestant church, declared that the AfD's views cannot be reconciled with a Christian moral compass and that hounding against Islam is unacceptable. He declared that he was taking a strong stance against the AfD's own 'fundamentalism'. Likewise, for Josef Schuster, President of the Central Council of Jews, the AfD's positions on Islam are 'unconstitutional' (evangelisch 2017).

Self-Fulling Prophecy or Political Prudence?

To conclude, the preceding discussion indicates that the Alternative for Germany embraced central tenets of Huntington's 'clash of civilizations' thesis to mobilize a substantial part of German society. In this way, 25 years on, the 'clash of civilizations' remains a relevant topic for scholarly debate and political analysis. By drawing on Huntington's reductionist conceptualization of conflict originating from Islam, the AfD continues to activate political capital. In particular, the humanitarian gesture made by the German government to welcome Syrian refugees helped the party bolster the perception that the country was under threat. As such, the AfD was able to enter the Bundestag as the third largest party and main oppositional faction in September 2017. To this extent, Huntington provided some bearing on the forces of 'civilization rallying' by populist forces. Critically, the CoC has also, even if unwittingly, provided the AfD with fodder to drive a self-fulfilling prophecy: Germany, at the core of the West, is under threat from radical Islam. It is here that Huntington's theory and the party's manifesto and political discourse pander more to the electorate's perception than conform with reality.

Theory and party, this chapter has argued, are equally problematic in their use of oversimplified categories, essentialist understandings of complex political phenomena, as well as their spurious and selective use of evidence to make their claims. Perhaps most troubling, they thereby perpetuate a divisive worldview of us versus them. An understanding that the West is under siege by radical Islam has provided the AfD with a tool to drive a nationalist agenda, just as much as it offered Huntington a stand-in enemy for the evaporating communist threat of the post-Cold War era. The AfD understands and justifies its approach as politically prudent. Still, the inherent danger with this approach is similar to that which has been made against Huntington. The CoC and AfD are thus usefully understood as two sides of the same coin: they construct a conflict scenario for which only policies of containment and restriction are offered as solutions. What both misjudge is that unbridled intolerance and opposing differences are at the root of every extremism. In this moment of populist resurgence with the AfD in Germany, under the Trump administration in the US, the National Front in France, the Party for Freedom in the Netherlands, Jobbik in Hungary and elsewhere, the question becomes not whether Islam is an inherent threat to stability but whether radicalization within diverse cultures is at the heart of whipping up the very conflict they seek to end. In the final analysis then, and to respond to this chapter's title, the AfD is not an appropriate alternative for Germany.

References

AfD. 2017. "Programm für Deutschland." *Alternative für Deutschland*. https:// www.afd.de/wp-content/uploads/sites/111/2017/06/2017-06-01_AfD-Bundestagswahlprogramm_Onlinefassung.pdf Accessed 03 November 2017.

AfD. 2017. "Mut zur Wahrheit."*Alternative für Deutschland*. www. alternativefuer.de/program-hintergrund/mut-zur-wahrheit Accessed 03 November 2017.

BBC. 2016. "'Nazi word' revived by German AfD chief." *British Broadcasting Corporation*, 12 September. http://www.bbc.com/news/world-europe-37337927 Accessed 03 November 2017.

Bundeszentrale für politische Bildung. 2017. "Alternative für Deutschland." *Bundeszentrale für politische Bildung*, 06 May. http://www.bpb.de/politik/ grundfragen/parteien-in-deutschland/211108/afd Accessed 03 November 2017.

Chiozza, G. 2002. "Is there a clash of civilizations? Evidence from patterns of international conflict involvement, 1946–97." *Journal of peace research 39*(6): 711–734.

Die Linke. 2017. "Stoppt die AfD! Linke Antworten auf die Gefahr von rechts." Accessed 03 November 2017. http://www.dielinke-nrw.de/fileadmin/kundendaten/www.dielinke-nrw.de/pdf/Dowloadbereich/AfD-Broschuere_A6_170410b.pdf

evangelisch. 2016. "Empörung über die AfD."*evangelisch*, 02 May. https://www.evangelisch.de/inhalte/134173/02-05-2016/empoerung-ueber-die-afd Accessed 03 November 2017.

Handelsblatt. 2016. "Der Islam gehört nicht zu Deutschland." *Handelsblatt*, 23 May. http://www.handelsblatt.com/politik/deutschland/afd-und-islam-der-islam-gehoert-nicht-zu-deutschland-/13628828.html Accessed 03 November 2017.

Henderson, E. A. and R. Tucker. 2001."Clear and present strangers: The clash of civilizations and international conflict." *International Studies Quarterly 45*(2): 317–338.

Huntington, S. 1993. "The Clash of Civilizations?." *Foreign Affairs 72*(3): 22–49.

Ipsos. 2016. "The Perils of Perception." *Ipsos*. https://www.ipsos.com/sites/default/files/2016-12/Perils-of-perception-2016.pdf Accessed 03 November 2017.

Katzenstein, P. 2009. *Civilizations in World Politics: Plural and Pluralist Perspectives*. Routledge.

Leif, T. 2017. "AfD-Vize wil Islam Grundrecht entziehen." *Tagesschau,* April 20. https://www.tagesschau.de/inland/glaser-afd-islam-religionsfreiheit-101.html

Niedermayer, O. 2013. "Eine neue Konkurrentin im Parteiensystem? Die Alternative für Deutschland." In *Die Parteien nach der Bundestagswahl*, edited by O. Niedermayer, 175–207. Springer Fachmedien Wiesbaden.

Patriotische Plattform. 2014. "Stellungnahme der Patriotischen Plattform: AfD muß sich gegen Islamisierung des Abendlandes aussprechen!" *Patriotische Plattform*, 09 December. http://patriotische-plattform.de/blog/2014/12/09/ stellungnahme-der-patriotischen-plattform-afd-muss-sich-gegen-islamisierung-des-abendlandes-aussprechen/ Accessed 03 November 2017.

Russett, B. M., J. R. O'neal and M. Cox. 2000. "Clash of civilizations, or realism and liberalism déjà vu? Some evidence." *Journal of Peace Research 37*(5): 583-608.

Said, E. 2001. "The clash of ignorance." *The Nation* 22.

Stichs, A. 2016. Wie viele Muslime leben in Deutschland? Eine Hochrechnung über die Anzahl der Muslime in Deutschland zum Stand 31. Dezember 2015 Im Auftrag der Deutschen Islam Konferenz (Nuremberg: Federal Office for Migration and Refugees).

SPD. 2017. "Faktencheck: Was ist dran an der Islamkritik der AfD?." *SPD*. https://www.spd.de/standpunkte/fuer-unser-land-menschlich-und-weltoffen/ faktencheck-was-ist-dran-an-der-islamkritik-der-afd/ Accessed 03 November 2017.

Tagesschau. 2017. "Afd-Vize fordert Einreisestopp für Muslime." *Tagesschau*, 04 March. https://www.tagesschau.de/inland/gauland-einreiseverbot-101.html Accessed 03 November 2017.

Taub, A. and M. Fisher. 2017. "Germany's Extreme Right Challenges Guilt over Nazi Past." *The New York Times*, 17 January. https://www.nytimes. com/2017/01/18/world/europe/germany-afd-alternative-bjorn-hocke.html Accessed 03 November 2017.

Note on Indexing

E-IR's publications do not feature indexes. If you are reading this book in paperback and want to find a particular word or phrase you can do so by downloading a free PDF version of this book from the E-IR website.

View the e-book in any standard PDF reader such as Adobe Acrobat Reader (pc) or Preview (mac) and enter your search terms in the search box. You can then navigate through the search results and find what you are looking for. In practice, this method can prove much more targeted and effective than consulting an index.

If you are using apps (or devices) to read our e-books, you should also find word search functionality in those.

You can find all of our e-books at: http://www.e-ir.info/publications

www.ingramcontent.com/pod-product-compliance
Lightning Source LLC
Chambersburg PA
CBHW070933030426
42336CB00014BA/2652